# Coaching for Performance

# Fourth Edition

The business agenda at the start of the twenty-first century focuses on working with change and developing people's potential and performance. The *People Skills for Professionals* series brings this leading theme to life with a practical range of professional development and human resource guides for anyone who wants to get the best from their people.

*Other titles in the Series*

COACHING CLUES
Real Stories, Powerful Solutions,
Practical Tools
*Marian J. Thier*

MEDIATION FOR MANAGERS
Getting Beyond Conflict to Performance
*John Crawley and Katherine Graham*

LEADING YOUR TEAM
How to Involve and Inspire Teams
Second edition
*Andrew Leigh and Michael Maynard*

THE NEW NEGOTIATING EDGE
The Behavioral Approach for
Results and Relationships
*Gavin Kennedy*

MANAGING TRANSITIONS
Making the Most of Change
Second edition
*William Bridges*

NLP AT WORK
The Difference that Makes the
Difference in Business
Second edition
*Sue Knight*

# Coaching for Performance

GROWing human potential and purpose

The principles and practice
of coaching and leadership

## John Whitmore

NICHOLAS BREALEY
PUBLISHING

LONDON · BOSTON

This fourth edition first published by
Nicholas Brealey Publishing in 2009
Reprinted 2009 (twice), 2010 (twice), 2011 (twice), 2012 (twice), 2013 (twice), 2014 (twice), 2015

First edition published in 1992

3-5 Spafield Street
Clerkenwell, London
EC1R 4QB, UK
Tel: +44 (0)20 7239 0360
Fax: +44 (0)20 7239 0370

20 Park Plaza
Boston
MA 02116, USA
Tel: (888) BREALEY
Fax: (617) 523 3708

www.nicholasbrealey.com
www.performanceconsultants.com

ISBN: 978-1-85788-535-4
eISBN: 978-1-85788-409-8

**British Library Cataloguing in Publication Data**
A catalogue record for this book is available from the
British Library.

Printed in Finland by Bookwell Oy.

# Contents

Introduction   1

## Part I The Principles of Coaching   7

1   What Is Coaching?   9
2   The Manager as Coach   20
3   The Nature of Change   27
4   The Nature of Coaching   33
5   Effective Questions   44
6   The Sequence of Questioning   53
7   Goal Setting   58
8   What Is Reality?   67
9   What Options Do You Have?   79
10 What Will You Do?   85

## Part II The Practice of Coaching   93

11 What Is Performance?   95
12 Learning and Enjoyment   100
13 Motivation and Self-Belief   106
14 Coaching for Meaning and Purpose   118
15 Feedback and Assessment   123

16 The Development of a Team                                    134
17 Coaching Teams                                              142
18 Overcoming Barriers to Coaching                             148
19 The Multiple Benefits of Coaching                           156

Part III Leadership for High Performance                       165

20 The Challenge to Leaders                                    167
21 The Foundation of Leadership                                176
22 The Qualities of Leadership                                 186

Part IV Transformation through Transpersonal Coaching          199

23 Emotional Intelligence                                      201
24 Tools of Transpersonal Psychology                           205
25 The Future Focus of Coaching                                221

Appendix: Some solutions to the nine dot exercise             227
Bibliography                                                  229
Acknowledgments                                               231

# Introduction

In 1992 when I wrote the first, short edition of this book, there were hardly any other books on new coaching methods for applications beyond sport. My purpose was to define and establish the root principles of coaching before too many people jumped on the fledgling coaching bandwagon, some of whom might not have fully understood the psychological depth and potential breadth of coaching, and where it fits in the wider social context. Without that understanding, they could easily distort the fundamental methodology, application, purpose, and reputation of coaching.

*Coaching for Performance* became the definitive book on coaching methodology in human resource departments and in schools of coaching both in England and abroad, and now, while many other fine coaching books have added to the field of knowledge, by and large we all subscribe to a common set of principles. The coaching profession has expanded and matured beyond all expectations, and managed its start-up and early teething troubles with dignity and little pain. There are a growing number of professional associations of coaches and it is gratifying to see that, in the main, they are cooperating rather than competing. The largest of these, the International Coach Federation, has nearly 20,000 members worldwide. Accreditation, qualifications, standards, and ethics are being agreed and monitored in a very responsible way. Coaching has moved from a cottage industry to a well-respected profession and has several journals dedicated to it. Meanwhile this book is now in 22 languages, including Japanese, Chinese, Korean, Russian, and most European languages, and it has sold some half a million copies worldwide.

What's new in this edition?

In this edition I am retaining and reaffirming the sections dealing with the definition of coaching and I dig deeper to reveal its psychological roots and to eliminate the surrounding weeds. Poor practice in coaching leads to the danger of its being misrepresented, misperceived, and dismissed as not so new and different, or as failing to live up to its promises. My intention is to keep the record straight by describing and illustrating what coaching really is, what it can be used for, when and how much it can be used, who can use it well and who cannot.

Contrary to the appealing claims of *The One Minute Manager*, there are no quick fixes in business, and good coaching is a skill, an art perhaps, that requires a depth of understanding and plenty of practice if it is to deliver its astonishing potential. Reading this book will not turn you into an expert coach, but it will help you to recognize the enormous value and potential of coaching, and perhaps set you on a journey of self-discovery that will have a profound effect on your business success, your sporting and other skills, and the quality of how you relate to others at work and at home.

This fourth edition explains more fully the principles of coaching in lay terms and illustrates them with simple analogies, not only from business but also from sport. It also clarifies still further the process and practice of coaching by drawing on the experience gained from the countless hours of training that my colleagues and I have delivered to many thousands of participants in the years since the book was first published.

I have added chapters on the relationship between coaching and leadership and on leadership itself. I am frequently asked by coaches what they can do to maintain and raise their skill in their coaching work. My answer is to practice, practice, and practice, but with greater awareness of yourself and other people, and to be committed to your own continuing personal development. That is something I go into quite deeply in the new chapters on leadership.

Leadership for high performance

I have elaborated further on the significance to performance of emotional intelligence (EQ), on the emerging interest in spiritual intelligence (SQ), and how they both relate to coaching. Higher workplace expectations of staff and the frequency with which they seek meaning and purpose at work mean that coaches are expected to acquire greater skill in addressing these deeper life issues. I look at what those skills are and how they can be developed. Companies are also having to accept that their values and ethics are falling and in some cases failing under the scrutiny of their staff as well as their customers. Coaching is highly effective for uncovering true values and producing the alignment without which business performance can never be optimized.

Like education, motivation, and management, coaching needs to keep up with the psychological development and understanding of how people bring the best out of themselves. There is always a time lag between what is known in some circles and the full adoption by the crowd. That is unfortunately all too true in coaching. For example, sports coaching is still mainly based on behavioral psychology, too much workplace coaching is still limited to cognitive psychology, and many other coaches confine themselves to humanistic psychological principles that maintain that awareness itself is largely curative. The Inner Game, however, reflects transpersonal psychology, which emphasizes the principle of will, intention, or responsibility.

Transformation through transpersonal coaching

Transpersonal psychology was fathered nearly a century ago by Carl Jung and Roberto Assagioli, but they were far ahead of their time and met some resistance, exacerbated by references to spirituality, which is negatively associated with religion by some people. However, today there is more willingness to explore new avenues in life, and coaches need to get up to speed with transpersonal coaching. In this edition I walk further into the transpersonal field, although I want to avoid coaches assuming that all that transpersonal coaching can offer is in these pages, so I strongly recommend proper transpersonal coach training, which is increasingly on offer.

The future of coaching

I conclude this fourth edition with a chapter on the future of coaching, its role in the transformation of learning and workplace relationships, and the wider social and cultural context that gave rise to coaching in the first place. Coaching, and the principles on which it stands, are timeless and global. It is a significant bridge in the evolution from hierarchy to self-responsibility, from autocracy to true democracy, from quantitative consumerism to qualitative sustainability that is being expressed in every field today.

Throughout this book I more often use the masculine gender, not because I am sexist, which I am not, nor because I abhor the literary clumsiness of "he or she" and "his or her," which I do, but because it is men who need to heed its message most. On the coaching courses my colleagues and I run, women have consistently shown more natural ability to adopt a coaching philosophy. It is more in line with their style. My own coach is a woman, of course. Perhaps the advent of more and more women into senior managerial roles will help to establish the practice of coaching as the communication norm throughout business. I hope so, and I hope that some of them will find the coaching model in this book useful.

## GROW FOR IT!

As with any new skill, attitude, style, or belief, adopting a coaching ethos requires commitment, practice, and some time before it flows naturally and its effectiveness is optimized. Some will find it easier than others. If coaching is already your style, I hope this book will help you take what you already do to greater heights, or provide you with a fuller rationale for what you do intuitively. If it has not been your style in the past, I hope that the book will help set you on some new ways of thinking about management, about performance, and about people, and provide you with some coaching guidelines within which to begin your practice.

There is no one right way to coach. This book is no more than a map to help you decide where you want to go and to introduce you to some routes toward your goal. You will have to explore the territory for yourself, since no map can portray the infinite variety in the landscape of human interplay. The richness of that landscape can turn people management into a personal and unique art form with which to decorate, appreciate, and enjoy your place of work.

We are facing crises in many fields, environmental as well as economic. Traditional silo or linear thinking is no longer sufficient to cope with unpredictable emergencies. We need the capacity to take a whole-system approach that is a product of personal development, of moving from the old fear paradigm to one of trust and of recognizing that humankind is evolving both socially and spiritually. Individuals can evolve far faster than the collective if they decide to embark on a personal developmental journey. Given the leadership failures that are so apparent today, a little compulsory evolution would do our leaders no harm at all. In practice the coaching process fosters evolution at every stage, for evolution emerges from within and can never be taught in prescriptive ways. Coaching is not teaching at all, but is about creating the conditions for learning and growing. GROW for it!

# Part I
# The Principles of Coaching

# 1
# What Is Coaching?

*Coaching focuses on future possibilities, not past mistakes*

The *Concise Oxford Dictionary* defines the verb to coach as to "tutor, train, give hints to, prime with facts." This does not help us much, for those things can be done in many ways, some of which bear no relationship to coaching. Coaching is as much about the way these things are done as about what is done. Coaching delivers results in large measure because of the supportive relationship between the coach and the coachee, and the means and style of communication used. The coachee does acquire the facts, not from the coach but from within himself, stimulated by the coach. Of course, the objective of improving performance is paramount, but how that is best achieved is what is in question.

## THE SPORTING ORIGINS OF COACHING

The concept of coaching originated in sport, and for some reason we have tennis coaches but ski instructors. Both for the most part, in my experience, are instructors. In recent years tennis instruction has become somewhat less dogmatic and technique based, but it still has a very long way to go. Ski instruction has moved too, but less by choice than by circumstances. Snow boarding, and variations on that theme, was "owned" by young people who taught themselves in part because few traditional skiing adults could do it. Aside from that, young people today have had enough of being told by adults and they are remarkably adept at picking up new physical skills. Shorter carver skis are also far easier to learn on, so ski schools have had to adapt their methods to suit the client rather than themselves.

## THE INNER GAME

A coach recognizes that the internal obstacles are often more daunting than the external ones

The teaching of tennis, skiing, and golf was tackled over two decades ago by Harvard educationalist and tennis expert Timothy Gallwey, who threw down the gauntlet with a book entitled *The Inner Game of Tennis*, quickly followed by *Inner Skiing* and *The Inner Game of Golf*. The word "inner" was used to indicate the player's internal state or, to use Gallwey's words, "the opponent within one's own head is more formidable than the one the other side of the net." Anyone who has had one of those days on the court when you can't do anything right will recognize what he is referring to. Gallwey went on to claim that if a coach can help a player to remove or reduce the internal obstacles to his performance, an unexpected natural ability to learn and to perform will occur without the need for much technical input from the coach.

At the time his books first appeared, few coaches, instructors, or pros could believe his ideas, let alone embrace them, although players devoured them eagerly in bestseller-list quantities. The professionals' ground of being was under threat. They thought that Gallwey was trying to turn the teaching of sport on its head and that he was undermining their egos, their authority, and the principles in which they had invested so much. In a way he was, but their fear exaggerated their fantasies about his intentions. He was not threatening them with redundancy, merely proposing that they would be more effective if they changed their approach.

## THE ESSENCE OF COACHING

And Gallwey *had* put his finger on the essence of coaching. **Coaching is unlocking people's potential to maximize their own performance.** It is helping them to learn rather than teaching them. After all, how did you learn to walk? Did your mother instruct you? We all have a built-in, natural learning capability that is actually disrupted by instruction.

This idea was not new: Socrates had voiced the same concept some 2,000 years earlier, but somehow his philosophy got lost in the rush to materialistic reductionism of the last two centuries. The pendulum has swung back and coaching, if not Socrates, is here to stay for a century or three yet! Gallwey's books coincided with the emergence of a more optimistic psychological model of humankind than the old behaviorist view that we are little more than empty vessels into which everything has to be poured. The new model suggested we are more like acorns, each of which contains within it all the potential to be a magnificent oak tree. We need nourishment, encouragement, and the light to reach toward, but the oaktreeness is already within us.

If we accept this model, and it is only contested by some aging flat earthers, the way we learn, and more importantly the way we teach and instruct, must be called into question. Unfortunately, habits die hard and old methods persist even though most of us know their limitations.

*It may be harder to give up instructing than it is to learn to coach*

Let me extend the acorn analogy a step further. You may not be aware that oak saplings, growing from acorns in the wild, quickly develop a single, hair-thin tap root to seek out water. This may extend downwards as far as a meter while the sapling is still only 30cm tall. When grown commercially in a nursery, the tap root tends to coil in the bottom of the pot and is broken off when the sapling is transplanted, setting back its development severely while a replacement grows. Insufficient time is taken to preserve the tap root and most growers do not even know of its existence or purpose.

The wise gardener, when transplanting a sapling, will uncoil the tender tap root, weight its tip, and carefully thread it down a long, vertical hole driven deep into the earth with a metal bar. The small amount of time invested in this process so early in the tree's life ensures its survival and allows it to develop faster and become stronger than its commercially grown siblings. Wise business leaders use coaching to emulate the good gardener.

Universal proof of the success of new coaching methods has been hard to demonstrate because few have understood and used them fully, and many others have been unwilling to set aside old, proven ways for long enough to reap the rewards of new ones. Recently, however, as much through necessity as progress, employee participation, delegation, accountability, and coaching have found their way into business language, and sometimes into behavior too.

## INNER BUSINESS

Tim Gallwey was perhaps the first to demonstrate a simple but comprehensive method of coaching that could be readily applied to almost any situation, particularly in his book *The Inner Game of Work*.

Many years ago I sought out Gallwey, was trained by him, and founded the Inner Game in Britain. We soon formed a small team of Inner Game coaches. At first all were trained by Gallwey, but later we trained our own. We ran Inner Tennis courses and Inner Skiing holidays and many golfers freed up their swings with Inner Golf. It was not long before our sporting clients began to ask us if we could apply the same methods to prevailing issues in their companies. We did, and all the leading exponents of business coaching today graduated from or have been profoundly influenced by the Gallwey school of coaching.

Through years of experience in the business field, we have built and elaborated on those first methods and adapted them to the issues and conditions of today's business environment. Some of us have specialized in teaching managers to coach, others have acted as independent coaches for executives and for business teams. Although coaches compete with one another in the market, they tend be friends and not infrequently work together. This in itself speaks highly of the method, for it was Tim Gallwey who suggested that your opponent in tennis is really your friend if he makes you stretch and run. He is not a friend if he just pats the ball back to you, as that will not help you to improve your game, and isn't that what we are all trying to do in our different fields?

Although Tim Gallwey, my colleagues in Performance Consultants International, and many others who now practice coaching in the business arena cut our teeth in sport, coaching in sport itself has changed little overall. It remains at least a decade behind the methodology of coaching that is virtually universal in business today. That is because when we introduced coaching into business 25 years ago, the word was new in that context and did not bring with it the baggage of a long history of past practice. We were able to introduce new concepts without having to fight old prejudices, and old practitioners, of old coaching.

That is not to say that we met no resistance to coaching in business; we still do at times from people who have remained strangely insulated from or blind to change. Coaching as a practice in business is here to stay, although the word itself might disappear as its associated values, beliefs, attitudes, and behaviors become the norm for everyone.

Finally, since I am defining coaching, I should perhaps mention mentoring, another word that has crept into business parlance. The word originates from Greek mythology, in which it is reported that Odysseus, when setting out for Troy, entrusted his house and the education of his son Telemachus to his friend, Mentor. "Tell him all you know," Odysseus said, and thus unwittingly set some limits to mentoring.

Mike Sprecklen was the coach and mentor to the famous all-conquering rowing pair Andy Holmes and Steve Redgrave. "I was stuck, I had taught them all I knew technically," Sprecklen said on completion of a Performance Coaching course many years ago, "but this opens up the possibility of going further, for they can feel things that I can't even see." He had discovered a new way forward with them, working from their experience and perceptions rather than from his own. Good coaching, and good mentoring for that matter, can and should take a performer beyond the limitations of the coach or mentor's own knowledge.

Some people use the term mentoring interchangeably with coaching. I quote from David Clutterbuck's book *Everyone Needs a Mentor*:

*In spite of the variety of definitions of mentoring (and the variety of names it is given, from coaching or counselling to sponsorship) all the experts and communicators appear to agree that it has its origins in the concept of apprenticeship, when an older, more experienced individual passed down his knowledge of how the task was done and how to operate in the commercial world.*

MENTORING

I'm afraid I disagree. The effect of coaching is not dependent on "an older, more experienced individual passing down his knowledge." Coaching requires expertise in coaching but not in the subject at hand. That is one of its great strengths.

POTENTIAL

Whether we coach, advise, counsel, facilitate, or mentor, the effectiveness of what we do depends in large measure on our beliefs about human potential. The expressions "to get the best out of someone" and "your hidden potential" imply that more lies within the person waiting to be released. Unless the manager or coach believes that people possess more capability than they are currently expressing, he will not be able to help them express it. **He must think of his people in terms of their potential, not their performance.** The majority of appraisal systems are seriously flawed for this reason. People are put in performance boxes from which it is hard for them to escape, either in their own eyes or their manager's.

To get the best out of people, we have to believe the best is in there – but how do we know it is, how much is there, and how do we get it out? I believe it is there, not because of any scientific proof but simply from having had to find reserves I did not know I had while competing in professional sport, and from observing how people exceed all their own and others' expectations when a crisis occurs. Ordinary people like you and I will do extraordinary things when we have to. For example, who would not produce superhuman strength and courage to save their child? The capacity is there, the crisis is the catalyst. But is crisis the only catalyst? And how long are we able to sustain extraordinary levels of performance? Some of this potential can be accessed by coaching, and performance can be sustainable, perhaps not at superhuman levels but certainly at levels far higher than we generally accept.

EXPERIMENT

That our beliefs about the capability of others have a direct impact on their performance has been adequately demonstrated in a number of experiments from the field of education. In these tests teachers are told, wrongly, that a group of average pupils are either scholarship candidates or have learning difficulties. They teach a set curriculum to the group for a period of time. Subsequent academic tests show that the pupils' results invariably reflect the false beliefs of their teachers about their ability. It is equally true that the performance of employees will reflect the beliefs of their managers.

For example, Fred sees himself as having limited potential. He feels safe only when he operates well within his prescribed limit. This is like his shell. His manager will only trust him with tasks within that shell. The manager will give him task A, because he trusts Fred to do it and Fred is able to do it. The manager will not give him task B, because he sees this as beyond Fred's capability. He sees only Fred's performance, not his potential. If he gives the task to the more experienced Jane instead, which is expedient and understandable, the manager reinforces or validates Fred's shell and increases its strength and thickness. He needs to do the opposite, to help Fred venture outside his shell, to support or coach him to success with task B.

**To use coaching successfully we have to adopt a far more optimistic view than usual of the dormant capability of all people.** Pretending we are optimistic is insufficient because our genuine beliefs are conveyed in many subtle ways of which we are not aware.

When and where do we use coaching and for what? Here are some of the more obvious opportunities to apply coaching at work:

APPLICATION

| | |
|---|---|
| Motivating staff | Appraisals and assessments |
| Delegating | Task performance |
| Problem solving | Planning and reviewing |
| Relationship issues | Staff development |
| Team building | Team working |

Coaching can be used proactively, during performance or in review

The list is endless, and the opportunities can be tackled by using a highly structured approach, the formal coaching session. The coach/manager can equally choose to retain a degree of structure but be less formal – superficially the discussion might sound like a normal conversation and the term coaching might not be used. Far more pervasive than either of these uses, and perhaps more important, are the continuous awareness and employment of the underlying principles of coaching during the many brief daily interactions that occur between manager and staff. In these cases we would not describe the interaction as coaching, and it might consist of no more than a single sentence – probably a question. However, the wording, the intention, and the effect of that sentence would be different. Here is an example:

Coaching can occur spontaneously in a minute or an hour-long session

EXAMPLE

An employee, Sue, is working on a task that had been discussed and agreed with her manager the previous week. She has a problem and goes to find her manager:

SUE    I did what we agreed but it isn't working.
MANAGER    You must have done something wrong! Do it this way instead…

No coaching there, but here is an alternative based on coaching principles:

SUE    I did what we agreed but it isn't working.
MANAGER    I just have to go and see George for a minute. See if you can find out exactly where and when the blockage occurs, and I'll be back to help you find a solution.

Ten minutes later when the manager returns:

SUE    I've got the solution, it's working fine now.
MANAGER    Great. What did you do? Did it affect anything else?
SUE    This was the problem, and I got round it like this… There are no other effects, I checked that out.
MANAGER    Sounds fine to me. See what you can do when you try!

The manager's sentence, not even a question this time although an implied one – 'See if you can find out exactly where and when the blockage occurs' – embraces the two key principles of coaching identified in Chapter 4, **awareness** and **responsibility**. Also in this brief interaction the manager showed no blame or irritation, presented himself as a partner in the cause, and at the end reminded Sue that she had solved the problem herself and that she is more capable than she thinks.

I have argued the importance of managers recognizing the potential that lies within everyone they manage and of treating them accordingly. It is, however, even more important for people to recognize their own hidden potential. We all believe we could do better to some extent, but do we really know what we are capable of? How often do we hear or make comments such as: "Yes, she is far more capable than she thinks"?

In bold below are three revealing questions that I invite you to ask and answer, before you read the answers underneath.

*We must see people in terms of their future potential, not their past performance*

**What percentage of people's potential manifests itself in the workplace on average?**
Individual answers given by delegates on Performance Coaching programs range from single figures to over 80 percent, but the average for any group turns out remarkably often to be about 40 percent.

**What evidence do you have to support your figure?**
The three most consistent answers are:

• The things that people do so well outside the workplace.
• How well people respond in a crisis.
• I just know I could be much more productive.

**What external and internal blocks obstruct the manifestation of the rest of that potential?**
The external ones most frequently cited are:

• My company's restrictive structures and practices.
• The lack of encouragement and opportunity.
• The prevailing management style of the company/my boss.

The single universal internal block is unfailingly the same, variously described as fear of failure, lack of confidence, self-doubt, and lack of self-belief.

I have every reason to suspect that this last block is true. It is certainly true for me. In a safe environment people tend to tell the truth about themselves. If lack of confidence and so on is perceived to be true, then in effect it becomes the case anyway. The logical response would be to put every effort into building employees' self-belief, and coaching is tailor-made for that, but many business people are anything but logical when the need for a change in management behavior is raised. They far prefer to hope for, look for, pay for, or even wait for a technical or structural fix, rather than adopting a human or psychological performance improvement, however straightforward it may be. There is another reason as well.

Building awareness, responsibility, and self-belief is the goal of a coach

Building others' self-belief demands that we release the desire to control them or to maintain their belief in our superior abilities. One of the best things we can do for them is to assist them in surpassing us. Children's most memorable and exciting moments are often the first occasions on which they beat a parent at a game of skill. That is why in the early days we sometimes allow them to win. We want our children to overtake us and we are proud when they do – would that we could be so proud when our staff do the same! We can only gain, through their greater performance and from the satisfaction of watching them and helping them grow. However, all too often we are afraid of losing our job, our authority, our credibility, or our self-belief.

## SELF-BELIEF

We build self-belief when we make decisions, take successful actions, and recognize our full responsibility for both our successes and our failures. However, nothing succeeds like success. In coaching it is paramount that the coachee produces the desired results from the coaching session, without fail. It is incumbent on coaches to understand this and ensure that they have helped the coachee to optimal clarity and commitment to action, including pre-empting all obstacles. Coaches are often afraid to pursue a coachee to certain success because they fear being seen as aggressive.

Nevertheless, coaching that does not result in success – and the coachee's own recognition of that success – will only cause a reduction in self-belief and undermine the primary objective of the coaching.

For people to build their self-belief, in addition to accumulating successes they need to know that their success is due to their own efforts. They must also know that other people believe in them, which means being trusted, allowed, encouraged, and supported to make their own choices and decisions. It means being treated as an equal, even if their job has a lesser label. It means not being patronised, instructed, ignored, blamed, threatened, or denigrated by word or deed. Unfortunately, much generally expected and accepted management behavior embodies many of these negatives and effectively lowers the self-belief of those being managed.

The underlying and ever-present goal of coaching is building the self-belief of others, regardless of the content of the task or issue. If managers bear this principle in mind and act on it persistently and authentically, they will be staggered by the improvements in relationships and in performance that result. You can find out more about coaching for self-belief in Chapter 13.

*The underlying intent of every coaching interaction is to build the coachee's self-belief*

Coaching is not merely a technique to be wheeled out and rigidly applied in certain prescribed circumstances. It is a way of managing, a way of treating people, a way of thinking, a way of being. Roll on the day when the word coaching disappears from our lexicon altogether and it just becomes the way we relate to one another at work, and elsewhere too.

## COACHING IS A WAY OF BEING

However, to help understand the fundamental principles of coaching, we will in the next few chapters be examining the more structured end of the spectrum. I hope that you will destructure the concept as you become more familiar with and practiced in the principles, and they become your own.

# 2
# The Manager as Coach

*A manager must be experienced as a support, not as a threat*

Here lies a paradox, because the manager traditionally holds the pay check, the key to promotion, and also the axe. This is fine so long as you believe that the only way to motivate is through the judicious application of the carrot and the stick. However, for coaching to work at its best the relationship between the coach and the coachee must be one of partnership in the endeavor, of trust, of safety, and of minimal pressure. The check, the key, and the axe have no place here, as they can serve only to inhibit such a relationship.

## CAN A MANAGER BE A COACH?

Can a manager, therefore, be a coach at all? Yes, but coaching demands the highest qualities of that manager: empathy, integrity, and detachment, as well as a willingness, in most cases, to adopt a fundamentally different approach to his staff. He will also have to find his own way, for there are few role models for him to follow, and he may even have to cope with initial resistance from some of his staff, suspicious of any departure from traditional management. They may fear the additional personal responsibility implicit in a coaching style of management. These problems can be anticipated and generally are easily coached away.

The polarities of management or the communication style with which we are familiar place an autocratic approach on one end of the spectrum, and laissez faire and hope for the best on the other.

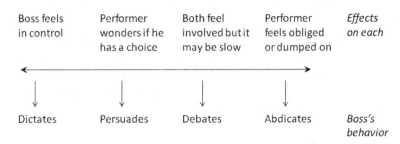

**TRADITIONAL MANAGEMENT**

| Boss feels in control | Performer wonders if he has a choice | Both feel involved but it may be slow | Performer feels obliged or dumped on | *Effects on each* |
|---|---|---|---|---|
| Dictates | Persuades | Debates | Abdicates | *Boss's behavior* |

When I was a little boy, my parents told me what to do and scolded me when I didn't. When I went to school, my teachers told me what to do and caned me if I didn't. When I joined the army, the sergeant told me what to do and God help me if I didn't, so I did! When I got my first job, my boss told me what to do too. So when I reached a position of some authority, what did I do? I told people what to do, because that is what all my role models had done. That is true for the majority of us: we have been brought up on telling, and we are very good at it.

DICTATES

The attraction of telling or dictating is that, besides being quick and easy, it provides the dictator with the feeling of being in control. This is, however, a fallacy. The dictator upsets and demotivates his staff, but they dare not show it or offer feedback, which would not have been heard anyway. The result is that they are subservient in his presence but behave differently when his back is turned, with resentment, with poor performance at best, maybe by downing tools or even by sabotage. He is anything but in control – he is deluding himself.

There is another problem with the dictating end of the traditional management spectrum: recall. Quite simply, we do not remember very well something we are told. The matrix below is an oft-used part of training folklore, but it is so relevant that it warrants being repeated here. It was a piece of research first carried out some time ago by IBM, but it was repeated, and the results confirmed, by the UK Post Office more recently. A group of people were divided randomly into three subgroups, each of which was taught something quite simple, the same thing, using three different approaches. The results speak for themselves. One issue they demonstrate that particularly concerns us, however, is how dramatically recall declines when people are only told something.

|  | Told | Told and shown | Told, shown and experienced |
|---|---|---|---|
| Recall after 3 weeks | 70% | 72% | 85% |
| Recall after 3 months | 10% | 32% | 65% |

I well remember showing this to a couple of parachute-jumping trainers who became very concerned that they taught emergency procedures only by telling. They hurried to change their system before they were faced with a terminal freefall!

PERSUADES

If we move along the traditional management spectrum to the right we come to selling or persuading. Here the boss lays out his good idea and attempts to convince us how great it is. We know better than to challenge him, so we smile demurely and carry out his instructions. Nicer maybe, if a bit phoney, and it gives the appearance of being more democratic. But is it really? We still end up doing exactly what the boss wants and he gets little input from us. Nothing much has changed.

When we get further along the line to discussing, resources are genuinely pooled and the good boss may be willing to follow a path other than his own option, provided it is going in the right direction. The late Sir John Harvey-Jones, interviewed about team leadership for David Hemery's book *Sporting Excellence*, said:

*If the direction everyone else wants is not where I thought we should go, I'll go... once the thing is rolling, you can change direction anyway. I may see they were right or they may realize it isn't the right place to be and head towards my preferred course, or we may both come to realize that we would rather be in a third alternative. In industry, you can only move with the hearts and minds.*

Attractive as democratic discussion may be, it can be time consuming and result in indecision.

The far end of the scale, just leaving the subordinate to get on with it, frees the manager for other duties and gives the subordinate freedom of choice. It is, however, risky for both. The manager has abdicated his responsibility, although the buck still stops with him, and the subordinate may perform poorly due to a lack of awareness of many aspects of the task. Managers sometimes withdraw with good intent, wishing to force subordinates to learn to cope with more responsibility. This strategy seldom serves its purpose, because if the subordinate feels obliged to take responsibility, rather than choosing to do so, his personal ownership remains low and his performance will not reflect the benefit of the self-motivation that the manager hopes to generate.

The majority of managers will position themselves somewhere between these extremes, but coaching lies on a different plane altogether and combines the benefits of both ends of the scale with the risks of neither.

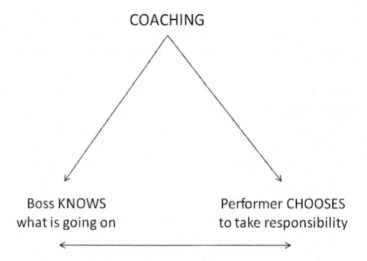

COACHING

Boss KNOWS
what is going on

Performer CHOOSES
to take responsibility

In responding to the manager's coaching questions, the subordinate becomes aware of every aspect of the task and the actions that are necessary. This clarity enables him to envisage the near certainty of success, and so to choose to take responsibility. By listening to the answers to his coaching questions, the manager knows not only the action plan but the thinking that went into it. He is now far better informed than he would be if he told the subordinate what to do, and therefore has better control of what is going on. Since the dialog and relationships in coaching are nonthreatening and supportive, no behavior change occurs when the manager is absent. Coaching provides the manager with real not illusory control, and provides the subordinate with real not illusory responsibility.

## THE ROLE OF THE MANAGER

What this discussion generates is: "What is the role of a manager?" Many managers too frequently find themselves fire-fighting, struggling to get the job done. By their own admission they are unable to devote the time they feel they should to long-term planning, to visioning, to taking an overview, to surveying alternatives, the competition, new products, and the like. Most importantly, they are unable to devote the time to growing their people, to staff development. They send them on a training course or two and kid themselves that that will do it. They seldom get their money's worth.

So how can managers find the time to coach their staff? It is so much quicker to dictate. The paradoxical answer is that if a manager does coach his staff, the developing staff shoulder much greater responsibility, freeing the manager from fire-fighting not only to coach more but to attend to those overarching issues that only he can address. So the activity of growing people represents enlightened self-interest rather than idealism that offers no added value. Sure, at times it will be all hands to the pumps and to hell with the niceties, but that is acceptable and accepted in a culture in which people feel cared for.

Managers often ask me when they should coach, or at least how they should decide whether to coach or tell. The answer is quite simple:

+ If **time** is the predominant criterion in a situation (e.g., in an immediate crisis), doing the job yourself or telling someone else exactly what to do will probably be the fastest way.
+ If the **quality** of the result matters most (e.g., an artist painting a masterpiece), coaching for high awareness and responsibility is likely to deliver the most.
+ If maximizing the **learning** is predominant (e.g., a child doing homework), clearly coaching will optimize learning and its retention.

In most situations in the workplace, time, quality, and learning all have some relevance all of the time. The sad truth is that in most businesses, time takes precedence over quality and learning is relegated to a poor third. Is it surprising that managers have such a hard time giving up telling and that business performance falls far short of what it could and should be?

If managers manage by the principles of coaching, they both get the job done to a higher standard and develop their people simultaneously. It sounds too good to be true to have

*A manager's task is simple – to get the job done and to grow his staff. Time and cost pressures limit the latter. Coaching is one process with both effects.*

*A coaching management style/culture results in getting the job done well for 250 days a year, developing people for 250 days a year, and a lot of self-belief*

250 days a year of getting the job done and 250 days a year of staff development per person, but that is precisely what the manager/coach does get.

# 3

# The Nature of Change

*If we do not change direction, we are liable to end up where we are headed*

The demand for change in business practice has never been greater than it is today. That the traditional culture of businesses has to change has been gaining acceptance intellectually for some years, but more recently the phrase "if they are to survive" has been added without much dissent. How has this come about? Why does what was good practice in the past not still hold good? Are we rushing into change for change's sake? How do we know it is going to be any better? And for how long?

There are plenty of cynical responses: "We have made all these grand changes in the past and they did not make any difference." "No sooner will we have made this change than we will have to change again." "Let's do nothing, it's just another new flavor of the month." These are the anxieties of many who are threatened by the inevitable plethora of uncertainties, but the questions and concerns are valid and we need to address them if we are going to manage change well.

There are also pragmatic reasons for change, such as increasing global competition forcing the pace toward leaner, more efficient, flexible, and responsive units. The pace of technological innovation frequently leads to managers finding that they have never learned the skills of the teams they employ. Globalization, demographic changes, the further integration of Europe, immigration, and the multiple effects of the internet and instant communication oblige businesses to change their ways.

However, by far the biggest challenge to hit business recently comes from the legal and social responsibility demands that follow the universal acceptance that climate change is both real and manmade. In future we can expect changes to come thick and fast and the economic downturn is only the beginning of worse to come. The conduct and the success of business are inextricably bound to the global social and psychological, environmental and economic factors to a far greater extent today than ever before. In addition, the commercial and financial demands made by businesses, and their power, mean that they also profoundly influence the surrounding culture, and those cultures are increasingly exercising their consumer power and hitting back.

## FROM WHAT TO WHAT?

So the culture of business has to change – but from what and to what? The answers to this, and most of the questions above, depend more on perspective than on consensus. Any new culture will have to deliver higher levels of performance, but also be far more socially responsible than ever before. No corporation is going to take the risks and suffer the upheavals involved in major change just for the sake of it, or merely to be nicer to employees, although perhaps it should. Culture change will be, and needs to be, performance driven, but the definition of performance is much broader today. Competition and growth are both losing their currency; stability, sustainability, and collaboration are gaining traction. Those companies and individuals who don't change their ways from what has been acceptable in the past to what will be acceptable in the future won't survive in our oversubscribed, fractured, and unstable markets. When the opportunities for promotion and pay increases are shrinking in most sectors, how does a business maintain, manage, and motivate its staff?

Expressions such as "our people are our greatest resource," "we must empower all our staff," "releasing latent potential," "downsizing and devolving responsibility," and "getting the best out of our people" have become clichés in recent years. Their true meaning remains as valid today as when they were first coined, but all too often they are hollow words. They are talked about far more than acted on. Coaching for performance is just what it says – a means of obtaining optimum performance – but one that demands fundamental changes in attitude, in managerial behavior, and in organizational structure. Coaching gives the clichés substance.

Most of the businesses we work with approach us because they are embarked on a process of fundamental change – or at least would like to be. They have recognized that if they are to achieve real performance improvement, their managers must adopt a coaching-based management style. These companies have already identified that coaching is the management style of a transformed culture, and that as the style changes from directing to coaching, the culture of the organization will begin to change. Hierarchy gives way to support, blame gives way to honest evaluation, external motivators are replaced by self-motivation, protective barriers fall as teams build, change is no longer feared but welcomed, satisfying the boss becomes pleasing the customer. Secrecy and censorship are replaced by openness and honesty, pressure of work becomes challenging work, and short-term fire-fighting reactions give way to longer-term strategic thinking. These are some of the characteristics of the emerging business culture, but each business will have its own unique mix and priorities.

NEW STYLE

However, there is another factor, more subtle perhaps but so pervasive that some find it hard to put their finger on. There is a growing awareness in ordinary people that is leading them to demand more involvement in the decisions that affect them, at work, at play, locally, nationally, and even globally. Decisions made by traditional authorities, governments, and other institutions, previously immune to challenge, are being called into question and sometimes brought to book by the media, pressure groups, and concerned individuals. Is this not

INVOLVEMENT

what was happening within the former Soviet Union and the Eastern bloc that led to the collapse of communism? In today's society it is easier to get a hearing than ever before, and cracks are appearing in impregnable citadels' dubious respectability. Those that have something to hide may hunker down and snarl, but the majority of thinking people welcome the changes, even if those changes do generate some feelings of insecurity. It matters not whether one sees this awareness as some evolutionary development or merely the result of a world shrinking because of its immersion in a sea of instant communication. It is happening either way.

## PUSH TO PULL

This demand for involvement and choice is a broad-based change in society as a whole and is often described as the shift from push to pull. What we mean by this is perhaps best illustrated by an example.

We all receive commercial and charitable junk mail that we don't want, resent, and regard as an intrusion. Some of us are on more mailing lists than others and some resent the deluge more than others. As you may have guessed, I am one of the latter! The advent of the internet gave us access to what we want when we want it. We have more choice. We download from the internet what we want, instead of continually having to bin what is pushed into our mailbox. Would it were that simple, of course. When I retrieve my emails or go on to the internet, I often find that the pushers have got there first and up pops some wretched dancing advertisement before I can grab the mouse.

I can recall when we only had two television channels in the UK; now we are spoilt for choice. We can select among hundreds of channels and even in some cases choose which camera to follow in a sports event. This again reflects the shift from push to pull. It is a result of the demand for choice in viewing, but we still have to put up with pushy commercials.

A similar shift is occurring in managing people. You used to be able to tell or push people to do what you want, but now they expect and demand to be treated differently. This is not a retrograde step, as some diehard pushers would have us believe. It is the evolving consciousness of our collective society, for which we should be grateful as it holds the promise of higher performance possibilities. Deep down people want choice and responsibility, and in many cases they are getting just that. Nevertheless, although executives talk about empowering people all the time, they still have plenty of push left in them.

**Responsibility demands choice. Choice implies freedom.** People, ordinary people, are beginning to recognize not only that this is what they want, but that it can be had to a far greater extent than previously understood even within our complex variety of social structures. Instead of feeling threatened, managers should realize that they can capitalize on this and give people responsibility, and that those people in turn will give of their best. This way everyone wins.

Companies often talk about getting rid of the "blame culture" – but they just as often take no action. Blame is endemic to business and endemic to a dictating philosophy. Blame is about history, fear, and the past. We need to refocus on aspiration, hope, and the future. Not only does the fear of blame inhibit even the most calculated risk taking, it blocks honest recognition, identification, and acknowledgment of the inefficiencies in a system. Appropriate corrections cannot be put in place without accurate feedback. Fundamental culture change will not happen if blame comes along too. But most businesses, and most people, will have great difficulty leaving it behind.

BLAME CULTURE

Blame evokes defensiveness – defensiveness reduces awareness

There is another good reason for increasing responsibility at work. Work-related stress is said to be reaching epidemic levels. A survey conducted by an independent research company in Minneapolis revealed that the leading cause of burnout was "little personal control allowed" in doing one's job and that this was prevalent irrespective of the state of the economy. This in itself suggests an urgent need for change toward working practices that encourage personal responsibility.

But what is the reason for this correlation between stress and lack of personal control? Self-esteem is the life force of the

STRESS

personality, and if that is suppressed or diminished so is the person. Stress results from long periods of suppression. Offering someone choice and control wherever possible in the workplace acknowledges and validates their capability and their self-esteem. Stress is thereby eliminated.

## FEAR OF CHANGE

However, for many people the fear of change, any change, looms large. This is not surprising when you consider that there is little we can do to prepare our children for the world they are going to live in. It certainly won't be as we have known it, but we don't know how it will be. Perhaps all we can hope to teach them is flexibility and adaptability to cope with whatever will be.

## CHANGE AS THE NORM

Most of what our great-grandparents taught their children would hold good throughout their lives. By and large they lived in a stable state, or at least stability was the accepted norm even if that was beginning to change! Most of us were brought up with that stable state mentality, but we are having to adapt to conditions that seem anything but stable. Our grandchildren will have grown up with change as their norm, so all they will have to cope with is the varying pace of that change. We are the generation struggling to adjust to the fact that change is now the norm because our teeth were cut on the illusion of stability. When much of what we know and love is in flux, full acceptance of personal responsibility becomes a physical and psychological necessity for survival.

# 4

# The Nature of Coaching

*Building AWARENESS and RESPONSIBILITY is the essence of good coaching*

Some readers may think by now that I have departed far from the subject of coaching, and that the role of the manager and the context of change are side issues. They are not. They are the context of coaching. If they are not understood, coaching becomes merely another tool in a kitbag of quick fixes. It is possible to coach another person to solve a problem or learn a new skill by diligently applying the coaching method and sequence described in this book without agreeing with the underlying coaching philosophy. The coaching may be competent and may achieve limited success, but it will fall far short of what is possible.

Some coaches have started that way. I remember one ski instructor we trained who was simply unready for deeper understanding. His manner was autocratic, dogmatic, and manipulative, but by systematically applying our method to skiing he got results that in turn served to convince him that offering the learner more choice was one key to unlocking all kinds of hidden potential. He soon changed his whole philosophy on and off the slopes. Not only did he go on to write a self-coaching ski manual and to design the best skiing program I know, he became an expert coach in sales training.

## RAISING AWARENESS

The first key element of coaching is **awareness**, which is the product of focused attention, concentration, and clarity. Let us return for a moment to the *Concise Oxford Dictionary*: aware means "conscious, not ignorant, having knowledge." I prefer what *Webster's* adds: "aware implies having knowledge of something through alertness in observing or in interpreting what one sees, hears, feels, etc." Like our eyesight or our hearing, both of which can be good or poor, there are infinite degrees of awareness. Unlike eyesight or hearing, in which the norm is good, the norm of our everyday awareness is rather poor. A magnifying glass or an amplifier can raise our sight and hearing threshold way above normal. In the same way, awareness can be raised or heightened considerably by focused attention and by practice without having to resort to the corner drugstore! Increased awareness gives greater clarity of perception than normal, as does a magnifying glass.

I am able to control only that of which I am aware. That of which I am unaware controls me. AWARENESS empowers me.

While awareness includes seeing and hearing in the workplace, it encompasses much more than that. It is gathering and clearly perceiving the relevant facts and information, and the ability to determine what is relevant. That ability will include an understanding of systems, of dynamics, of relationships between things and people, and inevitably some understanding of psychology. Awareness also encompasses self-awareness, in particular recognizing when and how emotions or desires distort one's own perception.

### AWARENESS LEADS TO SKILL

In the development of physical skills the awareness of bodily sensations may be crucial. In the majority of sports, for example, the most effective way to increase individual physical efficiency is for the performer to become increasingly aware of the physical sensations during an activity. This is poorly understood by the majority of sports coaches, who persist in imposing their technique from outside. When kinesthetic awareness is focused on a movement, the immediate discomforts and corresponding inefficiencies in that movement are reduced and soon eliminated. The result is a more fluid and efficient form, with the important advantage that it is geared to the particular performer's body rather than the "average" body that the book addresses.

A teacher, instructor, or for that matter a manager will be tempted to show and tell others to do something in the way he himself was taught to do it, or the way "the book" says it should be done. In other words, he teaches the student or subordinate his way and thereby perpetuates the conventional wisdom. While learning and employment of the standard or "right" way to do something will show initial performance benefits, the personal preferences and attributes of the performer are suppressed, making life simpler for the manager. The performer's dependence on the expert is also maintained, which boosts the manager's ego and his illusion of power.

> No two human minds or bodies are the same. How can I tell you how to use yours to their best? Only you can discover how, with AWARENESS

The coaching alternative of raising awareness surfaces and highlights the unique attributes of the body and mind of each individual, while at the same time building the ability and the confidence to improve without another's prescription. It builds self-reliance, self-belief and confidence, and self-responsibility. Coaching should never be confused with the "here are the tools, go and find out for yourself" approach. Our own normal level of awareness is relatively low. Left to our own devices we are liable to take an age to reinvent the wheel and/or to develop only partially effective methods that can consolidate into bad habits. So the awareness-raising function of the expert coach is indispensable – at least until or unless we develop the skill of self-coaching, which opens the door to continuous self-improvement and self-discovery.

> If there was only the "right" way to do something, Fosbury would never have flopped and Björn Borg would never have won Wimbledon

What we need to increase our awareness of will vary. Each activity is geared to different parts of ourselves. Sport is primarily physical, but some sports are highly visual too. Musicians require and develop high levels of auditory awareness. Sculptors and magicians need tactile awareness, and business people require mental and people awareness but certainly other areas too.

Although all this explanation of awareness may seem daunting at first, it is something that develops quickly through simple practice and application, and through being coached. It is perhaps easier to relate to the following lay definitions:

+ Awareness is knowing what is happening around you.
+ Self-awareness is knowing what you are experiencing.

INPUT

Another term may add to our understanding of what we mean by awareness: input. Every human activity can be reduced to input — process — output.

For example, when you drive to work you receive input in the form of other traffic movements, road and weather conditions, changing speed and spatial relationships, the sounds of your engine, your instruments, and the comfort, tension, or tiredness in your body. This is all input that you may welcome, reject, take on board sufficiently, receive in its intricate detail, or not even notice save for its major elements.

You may consciously be aware of your driving, or unconsciously acquire the input necessary to drive safely to work while you listen to the *Today Programme* on the radio. Either way you are receiving input. Better drivers will receive a higher quality and quantity of input, which provides them with more accurate and detailed information that they process and act on to produce the appropriate output, the speed and position of the vehicle on the road. However good you are at processing the input received and acting on it, the quality of your output will depend on the quality and quantity of the input. Awareness raising is the act of sharpening the acuity of our input receptors, often tuning our senses but also engaging our brain.

While high awareness is vital for high performance, we are blessed with a mechanism that continually seeks to lower our awareness to the level of "just enough to get by." While this sounds unfortunate, it is in fact essential if we are to avoid getting into input overload. The downside is that if we do not raise our awareness and that of those with whom we work, we will deliver output at a minimal level. The skill of the coach is to raise and sustain awareness at the appropriate level and in those areas where it is required.

On our courses we define awareness as **high-quality relevant input**. We could add the word **self-generated** before it, but in a sense that is already implied because input will simply not be high quality unless it is self-generated. The act of becoming engaged in something itself provides the quality. Consider the poverty of the image you receive if I say "The flowers out there are red," compared to the input you get when I ask you "What color are the flowers out there?" and you are compelled to see for yourself. Better still if I ask what tone or shade of red they are. One way gives a standard flower image, the other a detailed explosion of life in myriad subtle shades of red as it is at a particular instant. It is unique. In 15 minutes it will be different, for the sun will have moved. It will never be quite the same again. So self-generated input is infinitely richer, more immediate, more real.

*Higher than normal focused attention leads to higher than normal performance*

Another word that characterizes awareness is feedback – feedback from the environment, from your body, from your actions, from the equipment you are using, as opposed to feedback from other people.

*Change follows naturally and unforced once quality feedback or input is received*

## RESPONSIBILITY

**Responsibility** is the other key concept or goal of coaching. In the last chapter I raised the issue of the relationship between business culture change and a growing concern for accountability and responsibility, both collectively and individually. Responsibility is also crucial for high performance. When we truly accept, choose, or take responsibility for our thoughts and our actions, our commitment to them rises and so does our performance. When we are ordered to be responsible, told to be, expected to be, or even given responsibility if we do not fully accept it, performance does not rise. Sure, we may do the job because there is an implied threat if we do not, but doing something to avoid a threat does not optimize performance. Feeling truly responsible invariably involves choice.

*If I give you my advice and it fails, you will blame me. I have traded my advice for your responsibility and that is seldom a good deal*

Let's look at a couple of examples.

BLAME

If I give you advice, especially if it is unsolicited, and you take the action but it fails, what will you do? Blame me, of course, which is a clear indication of where you see the responsibility lying. The failure might even be attributable as much to your lack of ownership as to my bad advice. In the workplace, when the advice is a command, ownership is at zero and this can lead to resentment, surreptitious sabotage, or ownership of the reverse action. *You gave me no choice; you damaged my self-esteem; I cannot recover that through an action of which I have no ownership, so I take responsibility for an alternative action that will damage you. Of course, that course of action may damage me too, but at least I will have got my own back!* If this (unconscious) sequence in italics seems exaggerated to you, let me assure you that there are millions of workers with bad employers who would acknowledge having followed that track at times.

CHOICE

Here is another example of the difference between the normal or imposed level of responsibility and high or chosen responsibility. Imagine a group of construction workers being briefed: "Fred, go and get a ladder. There's one in the shed."

What does Fred do if he finds no ladder there? He returns and says, "There's no ladder there."

What if I had asked instead, "We need a ladder. There's one in the shed. Who is willing to get it?"

Fred replies "I will," but when he gets there there is no ladder. What will he do this time? He will look elsewhere. Why? Because he feels responsible. He wants to succeed. He will find a ladder for his own sake, his own self-esteem. What I did differently was to give him a choice, to which he responded.

One of our clients had a history of poor labor relations. In an attempt to improve these I ran a series of courses for shopfloor supervisors. Although the company grapevine reported that our course was very enjoyable, the participants were invariably suspicious, defensive, even resistant at the outset. I recognized that their pattern was to resist anything senior managers told them to do. They had been told to attend the course, and they would resist that too.

To defuse this unproductive situation, I asked them how much choice they had had about attending the course.

"None," they chorused.

"Well, you have a choice now," I said. "You have met your obligation to the company – you're here. Congratulations! Now, here is your choice. How do you want to spend these two days? You can learn as much as possible, you can resist, you can be as inattentive as you like, you can fool around. Write a sentence describing what you choose to do. You can keep it to yourself, if you prefer, or share it with your neighbor. I don't need to know and I won't tell your boss what you do. The choice is yours."

The atmosphere in the room was transformed. There was something like a collective sigh of relief, but also a release of energy, and the vast majority then engaged at a high level of involvement. Choice and responsibility can work wonders.

These simple examples clearly illustrate how important choice is for the performance gain that occurs with full responsibility. That does not occur unless the person feels responsible. *Telling* someone to be responsible for something doesn't make them *feel* responsible for it. They may fear failure and feel guilty if they do fail, but that is not the same as feeling responsible. That comes with choice, which in turn demands a question. We will look at the construction of coaching questions in the next chapter.

> Self-belief, self-motivation, choice, clarity, commitment, awareness, responsibility, and action are the products of coaching

**Awareness** and **responsibility** are without doubt two qualities that are crucial to performance in any activity. My colleague David Hemery, 400-meter hurdler and 1968 Olympic gold medalist, researched 63 of the world's top performers from more than 20 different sports for his book *Sporting Excellence*. In spite of considerable variations in other areas, awareness and responsibility consistently appeared to be the two most important attitudinal factors common to all – and the attitude or state of mind of the performer is the key to performance of any kind.

## AWARENESS AND RESPONSIBILITY

## THE MIND IS KEY

The mind is key – but where is the key to the mind?

For his research, David Hemery asked each of the performers to what extent they thought the mind was involved in playing their sport. David wrote, "The unanimous verdict was couched in words like 'immensely', 'totally', 'that's the whole game', 'you play with your mind', 'that's where the body movement comes from'. And as a minimum, 'It's equal to the body.'" Top performance in business demands no less. The mind is key.

### THE MIND IS KEY

Attitude of mind

Knowledge          Experience
(technique)          (fitness)

Knowledge and experience may be the business equivalents of sporting technique and physical fitness. Neither guarantees a place at the top, and many successful people have proved that neither is indispensable. A winning mind is essential.

THE WINNING MIND

A decade or so ago technical ability and fitness commensurate with your sport were what coaches worked on. The mind was not universally recognized to be so crucial, but in any case that was what the performer was born with and the coach could not do much about it. Wrong! Coaches could and did affect the state of mind of their performers, but largely unwittingly and often negatively by their autocratic methods and obsession with technique.

These coaches denied their performers' responsibility by telling them what to do; they denied their awareness by telling them what they saw. They withheld responsibility and killed awareness. Some so-called coaches still do, as do many managers. They contribute to the performers' or employees' limitations as well as to their successes. The problem is that they may still get reasonable results from those they manage, so they are not motivated to try anything else and never know or believe what they could achieve by other means.

In recent years much has changed in sport and most top teams employ sports psychologists to provide performers with attitudinal training. If old coaching methods remain unchanged, however, the coach will frequently be unintentionally negating the psychologist's efforts. The best way to develop and maintain the ideal state of mind for performance is to build awareness and responsibility continuously through daily practice and the skill-acquisition process. This requires a shift in the method of coaching, a shift from instruction to real coaching.

*Coaching for awareness and responsibility works in the short term for achieving a task, or in the long term for a better quality of life*

The coach is not a problem solver, a teacher, an adviser, an instructor, or even an expert; he or she is a sounding board, a facilitator, a counselor, an awareness raiser. These words should at least help you to understand what the role implies.

## QUALITIES OF A COACH

On our coaching courses we ask participants to list the qualities of an ideal coach. The following is a typical list and one with which I agree:

• Patient
• Detached
• Supportive
• Interested
• Good listener
• Perceptive

- Aware
- Self-aware
- Attentive
- Retentive

Often the list also contains some of the following:

- Technical expertise
- Knowledge
- Experience
- Credibility
- Authority

## COACH AS EXPERT

I am less in agreement with these last five and I pose a "coach as expert" question: Does a coach need to have experience or technical knowledge in the area in which he is coaching? The answer is no – not if the coach is truly acting as a detached awareness raiser. If, however, the coach does not fully believe in what he espouses – that is, the potential of the performer and the value of self-responsibility – then he will think that he needs expertise in the subject to be able to coach. I am not suggesting that there is never a place for expert input, but the less good coach will tend to overuse it and thereby reduce the value of his coaching, because every time input is provided the responsibility of the coachee is reduced.

## THE PITFALLS OF KNOWLEDGE

The ideal would seem to be an expert coach with a wealth of technical knowledge too. It is, however, very hard for experts to withhold their expertise sufficiently to coach well. Let me illustrate this further with an example from tennis. Many years ago several of our Inner Tennis courses were so overbooked that we ran out of trained Inner Tennis coaches. We brought in two Inner Ski coaches, dressed them in tennis coach's uniform, put a racket under their arms, and let them loose with the promise that they would not attempt to use the racket under any circumstances.

Not entirely to our surprise, the coaching job they performed was largely indistinguishable from that of their tennis-playing colleagues. However, on a couple of notable occasions they actually did *better*. On reflection the reason became clear. The tennis coaches were seeing the participants in terms of their technical faults; the ski coaches, who could not recognize such faults, saw the participants in terms of the efficiency with which they used their bodies. Body inefficiency stems from self-doubt and inadequate body awareness. The ski coaches, having to rely on the participants' own self-diagnosis, were therefore tackling the problems at their cause, whereas the tennis coaches were only tackling the symptom, the technical fault. This obliged us to do more training with the tennis coaches to enable them to detach themselves more effectively from their expertise.

Let us look at the same thing with a simple example from a business context. A manager saw that her subordinate, George, did not communicate sufficiently with his colleagues in the next department, and knew that a weekly progress memo was the solution. Such a memo, however, would contain inadequate information so long as George's resistance to communicating persisted. Instead of being satisfied with George's agreement to send memos, the manager coached George to discover and let go of his own resistance. The lack of communication was the symptom, but the resistance was the cause. Problems can only be resolved at the level beneath that at which they manifest themselves.

A LEVEL DEEPER

It is hard, but by no means impossible, for an expert to be a good coach. Of course, expertise is invaluable for many other aspects of a manager's function, and the truth is that the manager is most likely to be an expert anyway. But take the case of a senior manager in an organization that computerizes a part of its operations. If he is a good coach he should have no difficulty coaching his staff to develop their computer skills further, whether he understands the new system or not. As soon as he does this, any credibility gap that may exist in the minds of some of his staff will disappear, and he will be able to retain command of that department. As skills become more specialized and technically complex, coaching is an absolute prerequisite for managers.

THE MANAGER – EXPERT OR COACH?

Our potential is realized by optimizing our own individuality and uniqueness, never by molding them to another's opinion of what constitutes best practice

# 5
# Effective Questions

*Telling or asking closed questions saves people from having to think*
*Asking open questions causes them to think for themselves*

In the previous chapter it became clear that it is questions that best generate **awareness** and **responsibility**. It would be easy if any old question would do, but it won't. We need to examine the effectiveness of various types of question. To do so I will use a simple analogy from sport. Ask anyone what is the most frequently used instruction in any ball sport, and they will tell you: "Keep your eye on the ball."

In all ball sports it is certainly very important to watch the ball, but does the command "Watch the ball" actually cause you to do so? No. If it did, many more of us would be far better at our sport. We all know that a golfer hits balls further and straighter when he is relaxed, but will the command "Relax" cause him to feel more relaxed? No, it will probably make him more tense.

If commanding a person to do what they need to do does not produce the desired effect, what does? Let's try a question.

+ **"Are you watching the ball?"** How would we respond to that? Defensively, perhaps, and we would probably lie, just as we did at school when the teacher asked us if we were paying attention.

- **"Why aren't you watching the ball?"** More defensiveness – or perhaps a little analysis if you are that way inclined. "I am," "I don't know," "because I was thinking about my grip," or, more truthfully, "because you are distracting me and making me nervous."

These are not very effective questions, but consider the effect of the following:

- "Which way is the ball spinning as it comes toward you?"
- "How high is it this time as it crosses the net?"
- "Does it spin faster or slower after it bounces, this time, each time?"
- "How far is it from your opponent when you first see which way it is spinning?"

These questions are of an altogether different order. They create four important effects that neither the other questions nor commands do:

- This type of question compels the player to watch the ball. It is not possible to answer the question unless he or she does that.
- The player will have to focus to a higher order than normal to give the accurate answer the question demands, providing a higher quality of input.
- The answers sought are descriptive not judgmental, so there is no risk of descent into self-criticism or damage to self-esteem.
- We have the benefit of a feedback loop for the coach, who is able to verify the accuracy of the player's answer and therefore the quality of concentration.

This leads one to wonder why all those sports coaches persist in giving such an ineffective command as "Keep your eye on the ball." There are probably two main reasons: they have never considered whether it works or not, because it has always been done that way; and they are more concerned about what they say than about its effect on their pupil.

## THE HEART OF COACHING

I have taken some time to explore this apparently straightforward act of watching a ball in order to illustrate by simple analogy the very heart of coaching. We must understand the effect we are trying to create – **awareness** and **responsibility** – and what we have to say/do to create that effect. Just demanding what we want is useless; we must ask effective questions.

Coaching provides proactive, focused thought, attention, and observation

Similar questions also focus attention and evoke clarity in business. "What is the current stock?" "What is the most difficult issue for you?" "When is the engineer going to arrive?" "In what way will this price change affect our most recent customers?" All these are specific questions that demand specific answers.

These examples are probably sufficient to convince you that **awareness** and **responsibility** are better raised by asking than by telling. It follows therefore that the primary form of verbal interaction from a good coach is in the interrogative. Now we need to examine how to construct the most effective kinds of questions.

## THE FUNCTION OF QUESTIONS

Questions are most commonly asked in order to elicit information. I may require information to resolve an issue for myself, or if I am proffering advice or a solution to someone else. If I am a coach, however, the answers are of secondary importance. The information is not for me to make use of and may not have to be complete. I only need to know that the *coachee* has the necessary information. The answers given by the coachee frequently indicate to the coach the line to follow with subsequent questions, while at the same time enabling him to monitor whether the coachee is following a productive track, or one that is in line with the purpose or company objectives.

## OPEN QUESTIONS

**Open** questions requiring descriptive answers promote awareness, whereas **closed** questions are too absolute for accuracy, and yes or no answers close the door on the exploration of further detail. They do not even compel someone to engage their brain. Open questions are much more effective for generating **awareness** and **responsibility** in the coaching process.

The most effective questions for raising awareness and responsibility begin with words that seek to quantify or gather facts, words like what, when, who, how much, how many. Why is discouraged since it often implies criticism and evokes defensiveness, and why and how, if unqualified, both cause analytical thinking, which can be counterproductive. Analysis (thinking) and awareness (observation) are dissimilar mental modes that are virtually impossible to employ simultaneously to full effect. If the accurate reporting of facts is called for, analysis of their import and meaning is better temporarily suspended. If we do need to ask such questions, *why* questions are better expressed as "What were the reasons...?" and *how* questions as "What are the steps...?" These evoke more specific, factual answers.

**INTERROGATIVE WORDS**

Questions should begin broadly and focus increasingly on detail. This demand for more detail maintains the coachee's focus and interest. The point is well illustrated by the exercise of looking at a square foot of carpet. After observing the pile, color, pattern, and perhaps a spot or a stain, the carpet will hold little further interest for the observer and his attention will begin to wander to more interesting things. Give him a magnifying glass and he will look again in greater depth and for longer before becoming bored. A microscope could turn that little piece of carpet into a fascinating universe of forms, textures, colors, microbes, and even live bugs, sufficient to hold the eye and mind of the observer transfixed for many minutes more.

**FOCUS ON DETAIL**

So it is in business coaching. The coach needs to probe deeper or for more detail to keep the coachee involved and to bring into his consciousness those often partially obscured factors that may be important.

How, then, does the coach determine what aspects of an issue are important, especially if it is in an area about which he is not particularly knowledgeable? The principle is that questions should follow the interest and the train of thought of the coachee, not of the coach. If the coach leads the direction of the questions he will undermine the responsibility of the

**AREAS OF INTEREST**

coachee. But what if the direction in which he is going is a dead end or a distraction? Trust that the coachee will soon find that out for himself.

If coachees are not allowed to explore avenues in which they have an interest, the fascination is likely to persist and cause distortions or diversions in the work itself, rather than merely in the coaching session. Once they have explored their interests, they will be far more present and focused on whatever will emerge as the best path. Paradoxically, it may also be valuable for the coach to focus on any aspect that the coachee appears to be avoiding. So as not to break the coachee's trust and responsibility, this avenue of exploration is best entered into by a statement followed by a question: "I notice that you have not mentioned... Is there any particular reason for this?"

## BLIND SPOTS

Golfers and tennis players might be interested in the physical parallel to this principle. A coach might ask a pupil which part of his swing or stroke he finds most difficult to feel or be accurately aware of. It is most likely that in this "blind spot" lies a suppressed discomfort or flaw in the movement. As the coach seeks more and more awareness in that area, the feeling is restored and the correction occurs naturally without resort to technical input from the coach. The curative properties of awareness are legion!

## LEADING QUESTIONS

Leading questions, the resort of many poor coaches, indicate that the coach does not believe in what he is attempting to do. The coachee will quickly recognize this, and trust and the value of the coaching session will be reduced. Better for the coach to tell the coachee that he has a suggestion rather than attempt to manipulate him in that direction. Questions that imply criticism should also be avoided, such as "Why on earth did you do that?"

## BE ATTENTIVE TO ANSWERS

The coach must be fully attentive to the coachee's answers to questions. Trust will be lost if he isn't, but also he will not know the best question to ask next. Questioning must be a spontaneous process. Questions prepared mentally before they are asked will disrupt the flow of the conversation and not follow the interest of the coachee. If the coach is working out the next question while the coachee is speaking, the coachee will be aware that he is not really listening. Far better to hear the person through and then pause if necessary while the next appropriate question comes to mind.

Most people are not good at listening to others; we are *told* to listen at school, not trained to or coached to. Listening is a skill that requires concentration and practice. Yet strangely enough, few people have difficulty listening to the news or to a good radio play. Interest holds the attention; perhaps we need to learn to be interested in others. When we really do listen to someone, or when someone really listens to us, how appreciated it is. When we listen, do we really hear? When we look, do we really see? We short-change ourselves and those we coach if we do not really hear and see them, and by that I mean maintain eye contact with them. Obsession with our own thoughts and opinions and the compulsion to talk, particularly if one is placed in any kind of advisory role, are strong. It has been said that since we were given two ears and one mouth, we should listen twice as much as we speak. Perhaps the hardest thing a coach has to learn to do is to shut up!

*"Are there any other problems?" invites the answer "No." "What other problems might there be?" invites more thought.*

What do we listen to and for? The coachee's tone of voice will indicate any emotion and should be listened to. A monotone may indicate repetition of an old line of thought, a more animated voice will indicate the awakening of new ideas. The coachee's choice of words can be very revealing: a predominance of negative terms or a shift toward formality or childish language has hidden meaning that can help the coach to understand and therefore facilitate effectively.

## TONE OF VOICE

As well as listening, the coach needs to watch the coachee's body language, not with the purpose of making glib observations but again to help with the choice of question. The coachee's high level of interest in the direction of the coaching may well be indicated by a forward posture. Uncertainty or anxiety in answers may be revealed by his hand partially

## BODY LANGUAGE

covering his mouth while speaking. Arms folded across the chest often indicate resistance or defiance, and an open body posture suggests receptivity and flexibility. I am not going to go into the many aspects of body language here, but one guide is that if the words say one thing and the body seems to be saying something else, the body is more likely to indicate the true feelings.

## REFLECTING BACK

So we have listening, hearing, watching, and understanding, and the coach needs to be self-aware enough to know which he is doing. However clear the coach may feel, it is worth reflecting back to the coachee from time to time and summarizing the points being made. This will ensure correct understanding and reassure the coachee that he is being fully heard and understood. It also gives him a second chance to check on the veracity of what he has said. In most coaching sessions someone needs to take notes, but this can be agreed between the coach and the coachee. When I am coaching I like to take the notes so the coachee is free to reflect.

## SELF-AWARENESS

Finally, a good coach will be applying self-awareness to monitor carefully his own reactions, of emotion or judgment, to any of the coachee's responses that might interfere with the coach's necessary objectivity and detachment. Our own psychological history and prejudices – and no one is free of either – will influence our communication.

## TRANSFERENCE

Projection and transference are the terms given to these psychological distortions that all those who teach, guide, coach, or manage others need to learn to recognize and minimize. Projection means projecting on to, or perceiving in, another person one's own positive or negative traits or qualities. Transference is "the displacement of patterns of feelings and behavior, originally experienced with significant figures of one's childhood, to individuals in one's current relationships." In the workplace one of the most common manifestations of this is authority transference.

In any perceived hierarchical relationship, manager/ subordinate or even coach/coachee, both parties' issues or unconscious feelings about authority will be operating. For example, many people give away their power to the designated authority – "he knows, has all the answers, is more advanced" and so on – and make themselves small and childlike in the face of it. This might serve the wishes of an autocratic manager for dominance and dependence, but it works against the objective of coaching, which is to generate responsibility in the managed.

Another common example of an unconscious transference reaction to authority is rebellion and covert sabotage of work goals. Individual transference will increase the collective frustrations and feelings of powerlessness wherever management style limits choice. One major motor manufacturer used to be able to assess the state of labor relations from the percentage of good parts dumped in the reject bins alongside the assembly line.

Countertransference, which is a further complication of transference, occurs when the person in authority, the manager or coach, himself unconsciously reacts to the transference from his own history by perpetuating the dependence or the rebellion. A good manager or coach will recognize his potential for this and compensate for the effects of all manifestations of transference by consciously working to empower the subordinate or coachee. If he does not, these distortions will creep into managerial or coaching relationships, with the long-term effect of seriously undermining what his management style is intended to achieve.

## COUNTERTRANSFERENCE

Here are a few questions that I consistently find to be helpful in coaching. You may want to accumulate your own from your coaching experience. Above all, they must be authentic.

## HELPFUL QUESTIONS

- ◆ "What else?" used at the end of most answers will evoke more. Plain silence, while allowing a coach to think, often evokes more too.
- ◆ "If you knew the answer what would it be?" is not as daft as it sounds, since it enables the coachee to look beyond the blockage.

Coaching questions compel attention for an answer, focus attention for precision, and create a feedback loop. Instructing does none of these

- "What would the consequences of that be for you or for others?"
- "What criteria are you using?"
- "What is the hardest/most challenging part of this for you?"
- "What advice would you give to a friend in your situation?"
- "Imagine having a dialog with the wisest person you know or can think of. What would he or she tell you to do?"
- "I don't know where to go next with this. Where would you go?"
- "What would you gain/lose by doing/saying that?"
- "If someone said/did that to you, what would you feel/think/do?"

# 6

# The Sequence of Questioning

*Goals, Reality, Options, and Will*

So far we have established the essential nature of **awareness** and **responsibility** for learning and for performance improvement. The figure overleaf illustrates the many-pronged, many faceted nature of the benefits that spread out from these very simple but powerful concepts. Following any line of arrows from top to bottom illustrates the sequence of effects.

We have also looked at the context of coaching, at the parallels between coaching and managing, and at company culture and change. We have explored the role and the attitude of the coach, and we have considered questions as the primary form of communication in coaching. We now have to determine what to ask questions about and in what sequence to ask them.

It is important at this point to stress that it is possible for coaching to be loose and informal, so much so that coachees do not know they are being coached. For the everyday management function of briefing and debriefing staff, nothing is better than coaching, but it should not be identified as such; it would just be managing. In this case coaching ceases to be a

FORMAL OR INFORMAL?

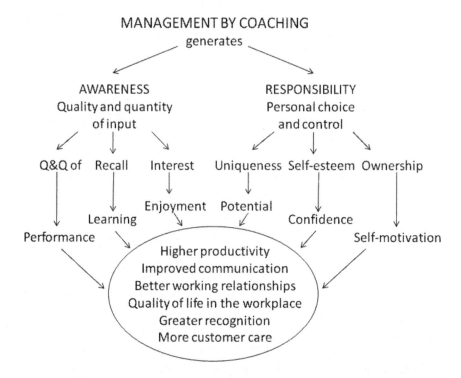

MANAGEMENT BY COACHING
generates

AWARENESS
Quality and quantity
of input

RESPONSIBILITY
Personal choice
and control

Q&Q of   Recall   Interest   Uniqueness   Self-esteem   Ownership

Enjoyment   Potential

Learning

Performance

Confidence

Self-motivation

Higher productivity
Improved communication
Better working relationships
Quality of life in the workplace
Greater recognition
More customer care

tool of management and simply becomes the way to manage people, in my opinion the most effective way. At the other end of the spectrum, a coaching session can be scheduled and structured in such a way that its purpose and roles are unambiguous. While the majority of coaching is of the former type, we will examine the latter in detail because, while the process is the same, the stages are more sharply defined.

## ONE TO ONE

For reasons of simplicity and clarity we will look at one-to-one coaching, although the format of team coaching or even self-coaching remains exactly the same. Both of these will be elaborated in later chapters. One-to-one coaching may take place between peers, between a manager and a subordinate, between an erstwhile teacher and a student, between a coach and a performer, or between a counselor and someone seeking his assistance. One-to-one coaching can even be used in an upward direction, although generally covertly, by an employee on his boss. After all, as no one gets very far by telling his boss what to do, coaching upward has a much higher success rate!

So the sequence of questions I suggest would follow four distinct headings:

- **Goal** setting for the session as well as short and long term.
- **Reality** checking to explore the current situation.
- **Options** and alternative strategies or courses of action.
- **What** is to be done, **When**, by **Whom**, and the **Will** to do it.

This sequence assumes that it is desirable to visit all four stages, which is usually the case when tackling a new issue for the first time. Often, however, coaching will be used to progress a task or process that has been discussed before or is already under way. In such cases coaching may begin and end with any stage.

It may seem strange to set **goals** before examining **reality**. Superficial logic suggests the opposite, as we surely need to know the reality before we can set any goal. Not so – goals based on current reality alone are liable to be negative, a response to a problem, limited by past performance, lacking in creativity due to simple extrapolation, in smaller increments than may be achievable, or even counterproductive. Short-term fixed goals may even lead us away from long-term goals. My experience with goal setting on team-training courses is that teams invariably set goals based on what has been done before rather than on what can be done in the future. In many cases they make no attempt to calculate what might be possible.

Goals formed by ascertaining the ideal long-term solution, and then determining realistic steps toward that ideal, are generally far more inspiring, creative, and motivating. Let me illustrate this very important point with an example. If we set about trying to solve a problem of heavy traffic volume on a strategic route by exploring the reality, we are likely to set goals based solely on relieving existing traffic flow, such as widening a road. This might actually run counter to a more visionary long-term goal, which would be formed by identifying the ideal traffic pattern for the region at some time in the future, and then looking at the stages needed to move in that direction.

So my suggestion is, in most circumstances, to use the sequence suggested above.

## MORE THAN GROW

This sequence conveniently forms the mnemonic G R O W, to which I will refer frequently. I must stress, however, that G R O W, without the context of **awareness** and **responsibility** and the skill of questioning to generate them, has little value. Mnemonics abound in the training business. There is S P I N, there are S M A R T goals, there is G R I T and there is G R O W coaching. These are occasionally presented or misperceived as panaceas to all business ills. They are nothing of the sort; they are only as valuable as the context in which they are used, and the context of G R O W is awareness and responsibility.

An autocratic boss might charge his employees in the following way:

My **goal** is to sell one thousand widgets this month.
The **reality** is that you did poorly last month with only 400 sold. You are a bunch of lazy so-and-sos. Our principal competitor has a better product, so you have to try harder.
I have considered all the **options** and we are not going to increase our advertising or repackage the product.
**What** you **will** do is the following…

He has followed the G R O W model to the letter but he has not asked a single question. He has created no awareness and, although he thinks he has threatened his staff into taking responsibility, this is not so, because they had no choice.

## CONTEXT AND FLEXIBILITY

The processes used by a coach, a counselor, a psychotherapist or a guru are similar: they build the awareness and responsibility of the client

If you get anything at all out of this book, let it be awareness and responsibility, which are more important than G R O W. Having said that, the strongest case for following the G R O W sequence with effective coaching questions is that it works.

It is, however, subject to recycling. What I mean by this is that one may only be able to define a vague **goal** until one has examined the **reality** in some detail. It will then be necessary to go back and define the **goal** much more precisely before moving forward again. Even a sharply defined initial **goal** may be recognized to be wrong or inappropriate once the **reality** is clear.

When listing the **options**, it will be necessary to check back to see if each of them would in fact move you toward the desired **goal**. Finally, before the **what** and **when** are set in concrete, it is crucial to make one last check to see if they meet the goal.

We will now take a deeper look at each one of these steps in turn and at the questions that best raise **awareness** and **responsibility** within each step.

# 7
# Goal Setting

*When I want to, I perform better than when I have to*
*I want to for me, I have to for you*
*Self-motivation is a matter of choice*

So much has been written about the importance and the process of goal setting that there is certainly no need for me to repeat it all in a book about coaching. Goal setting could fill a book on its own. However, I hope those who consider themselves to be goal-setting experts will forgive me if I run over those aspects of goal setting that we consider especially important for the coaching process.

## THE GOAL FOR THE SESSION

We invariably begin a coaching session by determining a goal for the session itself. If the coachee has sought a session, clearly it is he (or she) who needs to define what he wants to get from it. Even if it is the coach or manager who has requested the session to resolve a specific issue that he spells out, the coachee can still be asked whether there is anything else he wants from the session.

Questions like:

+ What would you like to get out of this session?
+ I have half an hour for this, where would you like to have got to by then?

* What would be the most helpful thing for you to take away from this session?

would elicit answers like:

* An outline for the month that I can develop.
* A clear idea of and commitment to my next two action steps.
* A decision on which way to jump.
* An understanding of what the principal issues are.
* An agreed budget for the job.

Now we come to the goal or goals related to the issue at hand, and here we need to be able to distinguish **end** goals from **performance** goals.

THE GOAL FOR THE ISSUE

* **An end goal** The final objective – to become the market leader, to be appointed sales director, to land a certain key account, to win the gold medal – is seldom absolutely within your own control. You cannot know or control what your competitors will do.
* **A performance goal** Identify the performance level that you believe will provide you with a very good chance of achieving the end goal. It is largely within your control and it generally provides a means of measuring progress. Examples of performance goals might be for 95 percent of production to pass quality control first time, for us to sell 100 widgets next month, or to have run the mile in 4 mins 10 secs by the end of September. Importantly, it is far easier to commit yourself to, and take responsibility for, a performance goal, which is within your control, than an end goal, which is not. An end goal should wherever possible be supported by a performance goal. The end goal may provide the inspiration, but the performance goal defines the specification.

The lack of an established performance goal played a major role in a notorious upset for Britain in the 1968 Olympics. Welshman Lyn Davies had won the gold medal in the long

PERFORMANCE GOALS ARE CRUCIAL

jump in 1964 and he, Russian Igor Ter-Ovanesyan, and US champion Ralph Boston were expected to share the medals. Along came a very erratic American, Bob Beamon, who in the very first round jumped some two feet beyond the world record. When one considers that the world record had risen by only six inches since 1936, this was a truly prodigious feat. Davies, Boston, and Ter-Ovanesyan were all completely demoralized, and although Boston got the bronze and the Russian was fourth, both were six inches behind their best. Davies, who was a foot behind his best, admits he was only focused on the gold, and that if he had set himself a performance goal of, say, 27 feet or a personal best and kept going for that, he would have won the silver. I wonder how demoralized other male swimmers became 40 years later in China, as Michael Phelps kept accumulating gold medals in every discipline up to his final tally of 11.

End and performance goals sometimes need to be topped and tailed by two other components, if not exactly goals. Take the example of Rebecca Stevens, the first British woman to climb Mount Everest. She gives lectures on her lofty achievements to businesses but also schools. You can be certain that after hearing her inspirational talk, many a schoolchild has run home and begged a parent to take them rock climbing or at least to the nearest gym with a climbing wall. "I am going to climb Everest" may be a childlike assertion, but it is also a personal dream, a vision that ignites action. Sometimes we need to remind ourselves, or be reminded by a good question, of what inspired us to start or continue to do what we want. We could call that a dream goal.

After some considerable climbing experience, Rebecca Stevens reached the skill level from which climbing Everest seemed to be a reasonable end goal; if climbing Everest can ever be considered reasonable! However, she still had a vast amount of work, preparation training, and acclimatization to do. Had she not been willing to invest herself fully in that process, Everest would have remained but a dream. "How much are you willing to invest in the process?" is a question I often ask in the goal-setting stage of coaching for any activity. I call this the process or even the work goal.

## OWNERSHIP OF GOALS

Although company directors may be free to set their own goals, all too often they pass goals down the line as imperatives not to be questioned. This denies ownership to those who are expected to meet these targets and their performance is likely to suffer accordingly. Wise directors will strive to maintain a healthy detachment from their own goals when they are seeking to motivate their managers, and will always encourage them to set their own challenging goals whenever feasible. But if they don't do this and a job is tightly proscribed, all is not totally lost, for the manager may at least be able to offer his staff some choice and ownership of how a job is done, who does what, and when.

Even if a certain goal is an absolute imperative, it is still possible to coach for ownership. I was discussing firearms training with a county police force. "How would it be possible to have trainees own the absolute, inflexible rules of firearms safety?" they asked. I suggested that instead of presenting them with these rules at the outset, they should have a discussion, using coaching, out of which the trainees would create their own agreed set of safety rules. The chances are that it would closely parallel the institutional ones. Where they were at variance, the reasons for the variation could be coached out of the trainees, with minimal input from the tutor. This way the trainees would have a far greater degree of appreciation, understanding, and ownership of the institutional firearms safety rules.

**COACHING FOR OWNERSHIP**

The value of choice and responsibility in terms of self-motivation should never be underestimated. For example, if the members of a sales team come up with a goal that is lower than the boss wishes, he should consider the consequences very carefully before overriding their figure and imposing his own. He may do better to swallow his pride and accept their figure. Insisting on his may well have the effect of lowering the performance of the team even though his target was higher than theirs. They may or may not consider his figure

**WHOSE GOAL?**

discouragingly unrealistic, but they will certainly be demotivated by their lack of choice. Of course, the boss has one more option if he is sure of his ground, and that is to start with the team's figure and coach them upwards by exploring and helping them to dismantle their barriers to achieving more. They then retain responsibility for the figure that is finally agreed.

## QUALITIES OF A GOOD GOAL

In addition to supporting an end goal, which is not in your control, with a performance goal, which is, goals need to be not only S M A R T:

- Specific
- Measurable
- Agreed
- Realistic
- Time phased

but P U R E:

- Positively stated
- Understood
- Relevant
- Ethical

and C L E A R:

- Challenging
- Legal
- Environmentally sound
- Appropriate
- Recorded

The point of a goal having most of these qualities is self-evident and needs no further elaboration, but a couple of observations may be in order.

If a goal is not **realistic** there is no hope, but if it is not **challenging** there is no motivation. So there is an envelope here into which all goals should fit.

It is very important to state goals in the **positive**. What happens if a goal is stated in the negative, for example "We must not remain at the bottom of the regional sales league"? What is the attention focused on? Being at the bottom of the league, of course! If I say to you "Don't think about a red balloon," what comes to mind? Or if I say to a child "Don't drop that glass, spill the water, make a mistake"? The example I like is from cricket, when a wicket falls and, just as the next batsman passes through the white picket fence, some wag says to him, "Don't get out first ball." He has the whole long walk to the crease to think about getting out first ball, and so he does. Negative goals can easily be converted into the positive opposite, for example "We are going for fourth in the league or higher" or "I am going to block the first ball however tempting it may be."

Goals must be **agreed** between all the parties involved: the boss who thinks he ought to set them, the sales manager, and the team who have to do the job. Without agreement, the vital ownership and responsibility of the sales team are lost and their performance will suffer accordingly.

We tend to get what we focus on. If we fear failure, we are focused on failure and that is what we get

It may appear preachy to suggest that goals should be **legal**, **ethical**, and **environmentally sound**, but each individual has their own code about these things and the only way to ensure employees' full alignment is to conform to the highest standards. Younger employees tend to have higher ethical standards than their older managers, who are often surprised and whose excuse is the usual "we have always done it that way." Besides, the new accent on accountability in business and throughout society, and the consequences of exposure by a whistle-blower or a consumer watchdog, surely outweigh any short-term gain that may tempt the unscrupulous! In *Sporting Excellence*, David Hemery quotes Sir Michael Edwardes as saying:

Coaching aims to eliminate both the external and the internal obstacles to achievement of a goal

*You will not get the TOP people working with you unless you have the highest standards of business integrity. If you value what you get out of corner cutting at £1000, the damage you do in demotivation of good people is minus £20,000.*

Some effort may need to be made to ensure that all goals are clearly **understood**, for all too often inaccurate assumptions may distort some people's perception, even of goals that they have been a party to creating.

## OLYMPIC GOAL

Perhaps the most striking example of good and successful goal setting I know also comes from the Olympics and from swimming, but from a decade before Michael Phelps was born. An American college freshman called John Nabor watched Mark Spitz win seven gold medals for swimming in the 1972 Olympics in Munich. There and then, John decided that he would win the gold in the 100 meters backstroke in 1976. Although he had won the National Junior Championship at the time, he was still nearly five seconds off the pace required to win the Olympics – a huge amount to make up at that age and over such a short distance.

He decided to make the impossible possible first by setting himself a performance goal of a new world record, and then by dividing his five-second deficit by the number of hours' training he could muster in four years. He worked out that he had to improve his time by one fifth of an eye-blink for every hour of training and he felt that was possible if he worked intelligently as well as hard. It was.

He had improved so much by 1976 that he was made captain of the American swimming team for Montreal and he won the gold in both the 100 meters and the 200 meters backstroke, the first in world-record time and the second as an Olympic record. Good goal setting! John Nabor was motivated by a clearly defined **end** goal, which he supported by a **performance** goal that was within his control. He underpinned this with a systematic **process** and this formed the dais on which he was to stand.

*Those who have to win, win a lot*
*Those who fear losing, lose a lot*

## A SAMPLE COACHING SESSION

Throughout the four chapters covering each segment of the coaching sequence I will illustrate the points made with the dialogue of a fictional coaching session with Joe Butter. Joe is

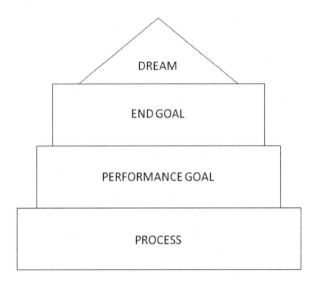

a senior account manager at a London advertising agency. His early meteoric rise through the ranks has slowed in the last two years, coinciding with the onset of middle age and the increase in his intake of food and drink, resulting in the expansion of his girth. Recently he tried to cut back and began taking exercise, but he was plagued by boredom, failure, excuses, guilt, and lack of commitment. He shares his concern with a colleague, Mike, who offers to coach him.

MIKE   Okay, Joe, what would you like to have by the end of this half-hour?

JOE   Some kind of plan to get fitter.

MIKE   For the rest of your life or what?

JOE   No, that would be too tall an order, and besides it might change once I get going. A realistic program for three months would be great.

MIKE   Let's look long term for a moment. What is the purpose of getting fitter for you?

JOE   I'm just feeling lousy about myself, and my work is suffering. I want to feel good again.

MIKE   Fine. How fit would you like to be by when?

JOE   I would like to lose 15 pounds or so, and within a few months be able not only to run upstairs and for the train without getting out of breath, but actually to enjoy running.

MIKE    Exactly what weight do you want to get down to, and by what date?

JOE    210 pounds by the end of the summer; that's about 15 pounds I have to lose.

MIKE    What day exactly?

JOE    20 September.

MIKE    Today is 19 February, so that gives you seven months.

JOE    Hmm! Two pounds a month, or maybe it will go faster to begin with.

MIKE    What do you want to lose by 1 June?

JOE    Ten pounds by then.

MIKE    You could do that by not eating and yet not be much fitter. How can we measure fitness?

JOE    I'll run 20 miles a week from the beginning of September onwards.

MIKE    Any particular speed?

JOE    No, I'll be happy to do it at all, and I'll know if I'm doing it satisfactorily.

MIKE    I don't care what speed, Joe, just give yourself a target speed. What will it be?

JOE    OK, nine-minute miles.

Joe now has a goal for the session, a long-term goal, and a halfway mark. His goals are specific, measurable, and probably incorporate all the qualities we recommend. Because there are no corporate imperatives in this case, he has complete and total responsibility for his own goals.

Now it is time to take a look at **reality**.

# 8
# What Is Reality?

*When the reality is clear, it brings the goals into sharper focus*

Having defined various goals, we need to clarify the current situation. It can be argued that goals cannot be established until the current situation is known and understood, and that therefore we should begin with **reality**. I reject this argument on the basis that a purpose is essential to give value and direction to any discussion. Even if goals can be only loosely defined before the situation is looked at in some detail, this needs to be done first. Then, when the reality is clear, the goals can be brought into sharper focus, or even altered if the situation turns out to be a little different from what was previously thought.

## THE SPORTING ORIGINS OF COACHING

The most important criterion for examining **reality** is objectivity. Objectivity is subject to major distortions caused by the opinions, judgments, expectations, prejudices, concerns, hopes, and fears of the perceiver. Awareness is perceiving things as they really are; self-awareness is recognizing those internal factors that distort one's own perception of reality. Most people think that they are objective, but absolute objectivity does not exist. The best we have is a degree of objectivity, but the closer we manage to get to it the better.

DETACHMENT

To approach **reality**, then, the potential distortions of both the coach and the coachee must be bypassed. This demands a high degree of detachment on the part of the coach, and the ability to phrase questions in a way that demands factual answers from the coachee. "What were the factors that determined your decision?" will evoke a more accurate response than "Why did you do that?", which tends to produce what the coachee believes the coach wishes to hear, or a defensive justification.

DESCRIPTION NOT JUDGMENT

The coach should use, and as far as possible encourage the coachee to use, descriptive terminology rather than evaluative terminology. This helps to maintain detachment and objectivity and reduces the counter-productive self-criticism that distorts perception. The diagram that follows perhaps best illustrates the point.

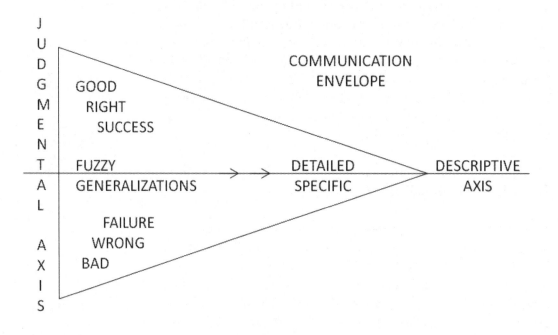

The terminology used in normal conversation, and many managerial interactions, falls generally toward the left-hand end. In coaching we try to move to the right. The more specific and descriptive our words and phrases become, the less criticism they tend to carry, and the more productive the coaching will be.

Care should be taken to remain close to the horizontal axis as often as possible. After all, there is not much I can do with the knowledge that my presentation was bad, but if I receive feedback that it was clearly structured, monotonic, brief, colorfully illustrated, and beneath the knowledge level of the audience, I am in a much better position to make improvements. Of course, some words such as colors or dimensions are purely descriptive; others acquire a vertical value only when some ideal is agreed. Yet others contain within them a degree of value in most usage (words such as lively or weak); but some are essentially evaluative, like good and bad or right and wrong. So, don't just tell a marksman that he missed – that will only make him feel bad. He wants to know that his shot was three centimeters above the bull and one and a half to the right if he is to make the correction. Description adds value, criticism usually detracts.

**Reality** questions, when applied to self, provide the most straightforward means of self-assessment. More about this and the way it can be applied for self-development is given in Chapter 14, but the skill of asking effective **reality** questions is paramount whatever the application.

If a coach only asks questions and receives answers from the normal level of conscious awareness, he may be helping the coachee to structure his thoughts, but he is not probing to new or deeper levels of awareness. When the coachee has to stop to think before responding, maybe raising his eyes to do so, awareness is being raised. The coachee is having to plumb new depths of his consciousness to retrieve the information. It is as if he is delving into his inner filing cabinet to find the answer. Once found, this new awareness becomes conscious, and the coachee is empowered by it.

DEEPER AWARENESS

**We have a measure of choice and control over what we are aware of, but what we are unaware of controls us.**

## FOLLOW THE COACHEE

The good coach will be inclined to follow the interest or chain of thought of the coachee, while at the same time monitoring how that relates to the subject as a whole. Only when the coachee is ready to leave each aspect of the issue should the coach raise anything that he deems to have been omitted. If the coachee seems to have wandered far off the track, a question like "In what way does this relate to the problem?" may bring him back or reveal a valid reason. Either way, it allows him to continue to lead the process.

By following the coachee's train of thought rather than asserting his own, the coach gains the coachee's confidence, because the latter's interest and need are being respected. For example, in the business context, say a senior manager, Alison, wants to investigate and correct an apparent problem in Peter's department. If she raises the problem at the outset, he is liable to feel threatened and become defensive. If that happens, his description of what has occurred will be distorted to make things look better than they are. However, if she lets him lead the conversation, will it ever arrive at the matter she wishes to address? Perhaps not initially, but if Alison bides her time, or more commonly bites her tongue, Peter may begin to feel safe enough to raise the matter himself. He will seldom have no idea that a problem exists, though at first he may not want to admit it to himself or others. When a subordinate begins to see his manager as a support rather than a threat, he will be much happier to raise his problems. When this happens, honest diagnosis and dialog are possible, leading to early resolution.

The blame culture that still prevails in the majority of businesses works against this, as it causes "false reality syndrome" or "I will tell you what I think you want to hear, or what will keep me out of trouble." Any corrections put in place thereafter will be based on a false reality. The wise manager starts with a more general investigation and follows the conversation of the coachee. The manager might assist the coachee with another, lesser difficulty, thereby establishing

Coaching may be requested by a coachee or a coach or it may follow a pre-planned schedule credentials as a support, rather than a threat. This approach is far more likely to lead in due course to the cause of the problem, instead of the symptom that is what is seen at first. **Problems must be addressed at the level beneath that at which they show themselves, if they are to be permanently eliminated.**

In the majority of business coaching scenarios, **reality** will concern the facts and figures, the incidents that occurred, the actions taken, the obstacles to be overcome, the resources and people available, and so on – things called up by and from the mind. However, if the coachee is learning a new physical skill, such as operating a tool of his trade, from a railway engine to a tennis racket, the coaching will also be focused on the senses: feel, sound, and sight.

USE THE SENSES

**Body awareness brings with it automatic self-correction.** If this at first seems hard to believe, just close your eyes for a moment and focus your attention internally on to your facial muscles. You will probably notice a furrowed brow or a tight jaw. Almost simultaneously with that awareness you are likely to experience a letting go, after which the brow or the jaw will be fully relaxed. The same principle applies to a complex physical movement. If attention is focused internally on the moving parts, the efficiency-reducing tensions will be felt and automatically released, resulting in improved performance. This is the basis of the new coaching approach to sporting technique and proficiency.

**Internal awareness increases body efficiency, which in turn results in improved technique.** It is technique from inside out rather than from outside in. Furthermore, it is technique owned, integrated, and unique to the body concerned, as opposed to someone else's idea of good technique to which you have forced your body to conform. Which is likely to lead to optimum performance?

The senses are one aspect of self-awareness. Another aspect is emotions, which have particular relevance to interpersonal problems at work or indeed elsewhere. Questions such as these will be used:

TAP THE EMOTIONS

- What do you feel when summoned unexpectedly to the boss's office?
- What emotions are you left with following the recent round of redundancies?
- What do you think you are afraid of?
- Where in your body do you experience tension?
- In what ways do you inhibit your potential?
- What is the predominant feeling you have when you know you have done a good job?
- Can you give me a rating on a scale of one to ten for your level of confidence in your ability to give a good presentation this afternoon?

ASSESS THE ATTITUDES

Self-awareness also needs to be brought to bear on our thoughts and attitudes in the moment, and on those to which we normally have less conscious access. Each of us brings with us, sometimes right from our childhood, long-standing beliefs, and opinions that will color our perceptions and our relationships with others. If we fail to acknowledge their existence and to compensate for their effects, our sense of **reality** will be distorted by them.

Trying hard or trying to change causes bodily tension and uncoordinated action, which all too often results in failure

**The interconnectedness of body and mind** Most thoughts carry an emotion with them; all emotions are reflected in the body; bodily sensations often trigger thoughts. It follows therefore that concerns, blockages, and inhibitions can be approached through the mind, the body, or the emotions, and a clearing of one tends to free the others, although not always. Persistent stress, for example, may be reduced by identifying bodily tensions; by evoking awareness of the feelings that fuel overwork; by uncovering mental attitudes such as perfectionism. It may be necessary to work on all three separately. Here I remind you of Timothy Gallwey's theme that the player of the Inner Game improves performance by seeking to remove or reduce the inner obstacles to outer performance.

LIMIT THE DEPTH

It is time for a word of caution. A coach may become aware of probing deeper into a coachee's hidden drives and motives than anticipated. That is the nature of coaching: it addresses cause, not merely symptom. Coaching may be more demanding than papering over the interpersonal cracks in the office with directives, but it is also more rewarding in terms of results. However, if you are inadequately trained in coaching or faint-hearted, stay out! If you suspect that a staff relationship problem has deep-seated origins, then it is better to bring in a professional with the necessary skills. One distinction between coaching and counseling is that coaching is mainly proactive and counseling is generally reactive. Another is that coaching generally addresses issues directly related to the workplace, but counseling skills are needed if the issue is ongoing or has childhood origins.

## REALITY QUESTIONS

The reality questions especially need to follow the "watch the ball" guidelines discussed earlier. Here they are repeated in slightly different terms. They are as follows:

- The demand for an answer is essential to **compel the coachee to think**, to examine, to look, to feel, to be engaged.
- The questions need to demand **high-resolution focus** to obtain the detail of high-quality input.
- The reality answers sought should be **descriptive not judgmental**, to ensure honesty and accuracy.
- The answers must be of sufficient quality and frequency to provide the coach with a **feedback loop**.

It is in this **reality** phase of coaching that questions should most often be initiated by the interrogatives what, when, where, who, and how much. How and why should be used only sparingly or when no other phrase will suffice. These two words invite analysis and opinion, as well as defensiveness, whereas the interrogatives seek facts. In the **reality** phase of coaching facts are important and, as in police investigation, analysis before all the facts are in can lead to theory formation and biased data collection thereafter. Coaches will need to be especially alert, listening and watching to pick up all the clues that indicate the direction of questioning to be followed. It must be stressed here that it is the coachee whose awareness is being raised. The coach often does not need to know the whole history of a situation, but merely to be certain that the coachee is clear about it. This is therefore not as time consuming as it would be were the coach to need all the facts in order to provide the best answer.

One **reality** question that seldom fails to contribute value is "What action have you taken on this so far?" followed by "What were the effects of that action?" This serves to emphasize the value of action, and the difference between action and thinking about problems. Often people have thought about problems for ages, but only when asked what they have done about them do they realize that they have actually taken no action at all.

## EARLY RESOLUTION

It is surprising how often the thorough investigation of **reality** throws up the answer before one even enters the third and fourth stages of coaching. Obvious courses of action that emerge in the **reality** or even on occasion the **goal** stage are often accompanied by a "Eureka!" cry of recognition and an extra impulse to complete the task. The value of this is such that coaches should be willing to dwell sufficiently long in **goals** and **reality** and resist the temptation to rush on into **options** prematurely. So, lest we do just that, let us revisit the coaching session that Mike is giving Joe.

MIKE   So much for your goals, Joe; now let's have a look at things as they stand. How much do you weigh?

JOE   225 pounds in my clothes.

MIKE   When did you last weigh yourself?

JOE   Last week sometime.

MIKE   Next door in the bathroom are some scales. Would you hop on them now?

JOE   ... Oh sugar! I'm 235 pounds.

MIKE   Do you eat excessively?

JOE   Yes, I'm a bit of a chocoholic and I do like rich food.

MIKE   Have you been eating a lot recently?

JOE    More than usual. I seem to when I am worried.

MIKE    What are you worried about now?

JOE    My health, middle age, and I feel a bit insecure about my job right now.

MIKE    Which bothers you most?

JOE    My health, I suppose, because I'm convinced that if I could get a grip on that, my state of mind and therefore my work would improve.

MIKE    Okay, let's stay with that for today, but in another session we could look specifically at your state of mind or your work. What do you eat too much of?

JOE    Chips and desserts.

MIKE    At every meal?

JOE    Most days both at least once.

MIKE    At home or when you're out? Lunch or in the evenings?

JOE    In the evenings at home, and when we eat out at least two evenings a week.

MIKE    With friends or with your wife?

JOE    Mainly just the two of us.

MIKE    Does your wife like to eat a lot too?

JOE    Not really, but she knows I enjoy it so she goes along with it.

MIKE    So you like sweets and chips, eat more when you are worried, and this is generally in the evenings and with the family. What about drink?

JOE    I sometimes have a beer at lunchtime, and I usually have a bottle of plonk in the evening.

MIKE    Exactly how many beers have you had in the last seven days?

JOE    Let me see… about 12.

MIKE    And the week before?

JOE About the same, if I'm honest.

MIKE    Shall we look at exercise now?

JOE    Okay. I have started running, at least.

MIKE    How often do you run and for how long?

JOE    I do about 15 minutes maybe twice a week.

MIKE    When did you run this week?

JOE    I didn't, I just felt too miserable.

MIKE   The week before?

JOE   On Sunday morning, just the once. I was going to again but my calves still hurt.

MIKE   Does the discomfort of running put you off?

JOE   Yes. Ankles, calves, thighs, heaving breath – I hate it.

MIKE   What other exercise do you take – walk, cycle, even run upstairs instead of taking the elevator?

JOE   No, but I do take an occasional sauna.

MIKE   How much do you think that helps?

JOE   It helps my guilt and it is not too strenuous.

Joe is now more honest with himself about the **reality** of his overindulgence in food and drink and of how minimal his exercise is. His wishful thinking or self-delusion is now grounded in reality. More importantly, he knows exactly where he is starting from.

Mike then takes him back to review his goal of 210 pounds, which is perhaps unrealistic in view of the fact that he actually weighs 235 pounds. However, Joe is so disgusted with the reality of his weight that he does not wish to alter the 210 pound target, even though this now requires a reduction of more than three pounds a month on average. Mike still considers it to be realistic.

Fortunately Mike offers to coach Joe on his running to try to reduce the discomfort he experiences, so this will give us the opportunity to hear an example of coaching a physical skill. They set out on a short run together, having agreed an easy pace and a goal of finding a comfortable running style, pace, and mental activity.

MIKE   Okay, let's just find an initial speed that feels relatively comfortable… What are you noticing in your body?

JOE   My calves feel stiff.

MIKE   Just place all your attention on your calves and tell me exactly what you feel in them?

JOE   A tightness down the back of them.

MIKE   When do you feel it? All the time in both calves or what?

JOE    No, just when I push off, and it is more on my right than on my left.

MIKE    Give your right calf a tightness rating on a scale of one to ten, with ten being as tight as you can imagine.

JOE    Actually it's now less, but it's about a five and the left leg is a three.

MIKE    What is it now?

JOE    It's down to a three.

MIKE    Keep monitoring it and tell me when it reaches two.

JOE    Both calves are a two now or even less. They feel great, but I notice my arms hurt as I swing them.

MIKE    Okay, just pay attention to the hurt in your arms and tell me more about it.

JOE    Hey, as soon as I started to pay attention to them I felt them relax, and I notice that I'm now holding them in a lower position.

MIKE    Is that more comfortable, then?

JOE    Yes, it certainly is.

MIKE    It actually looks more fluid as well.

JOE    Yes, I really feel I'm moving quite well. Normally by this point my breath is heaving, but I notice that I'm breathing quite rhythmically.

MIKE    Just follow your breathing for a while. Don't try to breathe differently, but notice the inbreath and the outbreath as it happens each time.

JOE    It's slowing down even more. I'll become a runner yet!

MIKE    What is the quality you would most like to find in your running?

JOE    You mentioned it and I'm beginning to feel it – flowing.

MIKE    Okay, rate how much you're flowing on a 1–10 scale.

JOE    Well, it was about four but it's already a six.

MIKE    Where in your body do you take your reading from?

JOE    My shoulders, funnily enough.

MIKE    What is it now?

JOE    It's an eight! I feel great!

MIKE    Yes, and we're back at base three minutes faster than you thought you could do it.

JOE    That's amazing. I feel I could do another 15 minutes, no sweat.

MIKE   You will before long. Well done. You see how focusing the attention internally clears up problem areas, leads to relaxation, and is so interesting that boredom is eliminated. It turns a chore into a pleasure.

JOE    You never even told me how to run more efficiently, but I seem to have found that flow for myself. That makes me feel good, and opens up possibilities in other areas too.

In coaching purely to learn or develop a physical skill on the field or in real time, the process we use, repeated in different forms of course, is complete at the end of this phase. The performance improvement takes place through the application of **awareness** during this **reality** phase, as it did for Joe. However, for the overall improvement of Joe's health and wellbeing, and for the furtherance of most business issues, which require planning, investigation, reviewing, and the like, there are two more phases to go.

# 9
# What Options Do You Have?

*When you are sure that you have no more ideas, just come up with one more*

The purpose of the OPTIONS stage is not to find the "right" answer but to create and list as many alternative courses of action as possible. The quantity of options is more important at this stage than the quality and feasibility of each one. The brain-stimulating process of gathering all the options is as valuable as the option list itself, because it gets the creative juices flowing. It is from this broad base of creative possibilities that specific action steps will be selected. If preferences, censorship, ridicule, obstacles, or the need for completeness are expressed during the collection process, potentially valuable contributions will be missed and the choices will be limited.

## MAXIMIZING CHOICES

The coach will do all he can to draw these options from the coachee or from the team he is coaching/managing. To do this he needs to create an environment in which participants will feel safe enough to express their thoughts and ideas without inhibition or fear of judgment from the coach or others. All contributions, however apparently silly, need to be noted down, usually by the coach, in case they contain a germ of an idea that may leap into significance in the light of later suggestions.

## NEGATIVE ASSUMPTIONS

One of the factors that most restricts the generation of creative solutions to business and other issues is the implicit assumptions we carry, many of which we are barely conscious of. For example:

+ It can't be done.
+ It can't be done like that.
+ They would never agree to that.
+ It's bound to cost too much.
+ We can't afford the time.
+ The competition must have thought of that.

There are many more. Note that all of them contain a negative or a dismissal. A good coach would invite his coachees to ask themselves "What if…?" For example:

+ What if you had a large enough budget?
+ What if you had more staff?
+ What if you knew the answer? What would it be?
+ What if that obstacle did not exist? What would you do then?

By this process, which temporarily sidesteps the censorship of the rational mind, more creative thought is unleashed and perhaps the obstacle is found to be less insurmountable than it seemed. Maybe another team member knows a way round that particular obstacle, so the impossible is made possible by the combined contributions of more than one person.

## THE NINE DOT EXERCISE

On our training courses for coaches we sometimes use the well-known nine dot exercise to illustrate graphically the self-limiting assumptions we all tend to make. For those of you who are not familiar with the exercise, or who have done it but may not remember the answer, here it is.

## NINE DOT EXERCISE

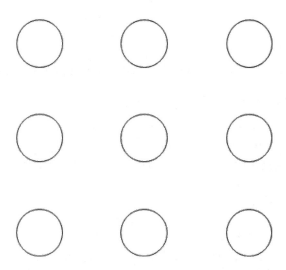

## Join the nine dots, using four straight lines *only*. Your pen must not leave the page and you may not repeat any line.

You may have remembered or realized that the assumption that has to be eliminated is the one that says, "You have to stay within the square." However, don't become too smug. Can you do it again with the same rules but using three lines or less? What assumptions are you limiting yourself with now?

Of course, no one said you had to draw your line through the middle of the dots, but I bet you assumed that. What about two lines, or even one?

No one said you could not tear the page out and roll it into a cone, tear it into three strips, or fold it like a concertina. What this has done is to break another assumption, the one that thought we only had one variable, the position of the lines. But who said you could not move the dots? Recognizing all the available variables will expand our thinking and our list of options. Breaking out of these self-limiting assumptions frees us to solve old problems in new ways. The key is to identify the false assumption; the resolution is then much more easy to find. (Several nine-dot solutions are on page 227.)

SORTING OPTIONS

**Benefits and costs** Once a comprehensive list has been generated, the **will** phase of coaching may just be a simple matter of selecting the best of the bunch. However, in more complex issues, as so many in business are, it may be necessary to reexamine the list by noting the benefits and costs of each of the courses of action. This should again be done by coaching, and it is here that some blend of two or more ideas may emerge as the optimum. Here I sometimes invite the coachee to note how much he likes each option on the list on a 1–10 scale.

**Input from the coach** What does the coach do if he has particular knowledge, skill, or experience of the matter in question and the coachee has not come up with what is, to the coach, the obvious solution? At what stage should the coach offer his expertise? Clearly, when he recognizes that the coachee has exhausted his possibilities. But how can he provide his input and still not undermine the coachee's sense of total ownership? Quite simply by saying, "I have another couple of possible options. Would you like to have them?" Very few coachees will ever say no, but they might ask the coach to wait while they complete a particular train of thought. Any suggestions provided by the coach should only be accorded the same importance as all the other **options**.

**Mapping the options** In the listing of **options**, the subconscious hierarchy (the more important things come first) that exists when a vertical column is made can be avoided by writing them randomly on a paper in the way a crossword expert solves an anagram.

Let us see how Mike, who happens to be a bit of a fitness buff himself, tackles the **options** issue with Joe, who clearly expects some prescription from the expert for his unhealthy condition.

MIKE    So what are all the different things you could do, Joe, to get yourself leaner and fitter?

JOE    I could run more often, or further, or faster.

MIKE    What else?

JOE    I could cut down my eating, and my drinking.

MIKE    What else?

JOE    I could eat fewer fatty foods.

MIKE    What other forms of exercise could you take?

JOE    Oh well, I suppose I could go to the gym.

MIKE    Anything else?

JOE    I could swim or I could even take up squash, which is something I've thought about at times. Or golf.

MIKE    What else could you do that requires no investment, no equipment, no clubs to join, just within your normal life?

JOE    I can't think of anything. I couldn't cycle, because I don't have a bike and I'm not going to buy one for that!

MIKE    What if you did have one?

JOE    I could cycle to work – and to the pub! I could actually walk to work and run up the stairs rather than take the lift to the fourth floor.

MIKE    Indeed you could. Is that it?

JOE    That's enough, isn't it?

MIKE    Would you like one more option to consider?

JOE    Sure, if you have one.

MIKE    How about weights and an exercise regime at home?

JOE    Yes, that's possible too.

Joe and Mike then examine the list and consider the advantages and disadvantages of these options. Golf is time consuming. Squash is a much quicker and more strenuous form of exercise, but it takes a little time to learn to get the best out of it. The nearest swimming pool is five miles away, but swimming is injury free. Together they explore the practicalities of certain diets and of being able to stay off drink in the business environment.

Lest you are thinking that this example of coaching is a little removed from the business context, you might consider the

FIT FOR WORK

following statement made by Sir Michael Edwardes in an interview with David Hemery for his book *Sporting Excellence*:

*I am always very hesitant about bringing an unfit, overweight person into a team; it suggests a lack of discipline. I am sixty and play squash three times a week and tennis once. I'm not overweight. My energy is greater than it was at fifty. I'm sure I'm fitter than my opposition and I think that is material. I wouldn't want anyone on my team who wasn't physically fit.*

Some people would consider such a statement politically incorrect – but that does not make it untrue. There is an irrefutable relationship between physical, mental, and emotional fitness, so why deny it?

Anyway, Joe is now aware of all the **options** and is pretty clear about their various pros and cons. Decision time has arrived.

# 10
# What Will You Do?

*Decision time and time for precision*

The purpose of this final phase of the coaching sequence is to convert a discussion into a decision. It is the construction of an action plan to meet a requirement that has been clearly specified, on ground that has been thoroughly surveyed, and using the widest possible choice of building materials.

The following set of **will** questions are applicable to the majority of coaching situations. Of course, the coach will add subsets of questions to clarify each of these points, but the principal questions form an effective backbone for this phase.

The demands of a managerial autocrat are often met with quiet resignation, resistance, or resentment, however diplomatically they are expressed. A coach, on the other hand, can bring a surprising degree of toughness into this phase of his questioning without causing any bad feelings, since he is not imposing his own will but activating the will of the coachee. Coachees always maintain choice and ownership, even if their decision is to take no action, and therefore they will not feel oppressed by hard questions. They might even be amused by the recognition of their own ambivalence. If they do feel pushed, it suggests that the coach is unconsciously revealing that he thinks the coachee *should* take a particular action.

I will now look at the value, the objective, and the best way to ask each of these questions.

• **What are you going to do?** This question is quite distinct from "What could you do?" or "What are you thinking of doing?" or "Which of these do you prefer?" None of these implies a firm decision. Once the coach has asked this question in a clear, firm voice, indicating that it is decision time, he may follow it up with a question like "Which of these alternatives are you going to act on?" In most coaching issues the action plan will incorporate more than one of the options or parts of the options combined.

The options have been only loosely defined. Now is the time for the coach to ask questions to clarify the detail of the chosen options. By far the most important of these will be:

• **When are you going to do it?** This is the toughest of all the questions. We all have big ideas of what we would like to do or are going to do, but it is only when we give it a time frame that it takes on a level of reality. And sometime next year is insufficient too. If something is going to happen the timing needs to be highly specific.

  If a single action is required the answer sought might be "at 10 a.m. next Tuesday, the 12th." Often both a starting time and date and a finishing date will be required. If the action to be followed is a repetitive one, then the intervals need to be specified: "We will meet at 9 a.m. on the first Wednesday of every month." It is up to the coach to tie the coachee down to exact timings. The coachee may wriggle, but a good coach will not let him off the hook.

• **Will this action meet your goal?** Now that we have an action and a time frame, it is important before we proceed any further to check that this is leading in the direction of both the goal of the session and the long-term goal. Without checking back, the coachee may find that he has wandered a long way off track. If this has happened, it is important not to rush to change the action, but to check if in fact it is the goal that needs to be modified in the light of what has come up since it was defined.

- **What obstacles might you meet along the way?** It is important to prepare for and pre-empt any circumstances that could arise that would inhibit completion of the action. Disruptive external scenarios might be looming, but internal ones could also occur, such as the faintheartedness of the coachee. Some people experience a shrinking commitment and just can't wait for an obstacle to appear and provide them with an excuse for noncompletion. This can be pre-empted by the coaching process.

- **Who needs to know?** All too frequently in business, plans are changed and the people who should be told promptly hear this only later and at second hand, something that is very bad for staff relations. The coach needs to satisfy himself that all the appropriate people are listed and that a plan is made for them to be informed.

- **What support do you need?** This is possibly related to the previous question, but support can come in many different forms. It could mean an arrangement to bring in outside people, skills, or resources, or it could be as simple as informing a colleague of your intention and asking them to remind you or keep you on target. Merely sharing your intended action with another person often has the effect of ensuring that you do it.

- **How and when are you going to get that support?** It is no good wanting some support but not taking the steps necessary to get it. Here the coach needs to persist until the coachee's actions are clear and certain.

- **What other considerations do you have?** This is a necessary catch-all question so that the coachee cannot claim that the coach omitted something. It is the coachee's responsibility to ensure that nothing is left out.

- **Rate on a 1–10 scale the degree of certainty you have that you will carry out the actions agreed** This is not rating the certainty of the outcome actually happening. It is a rating of the coachee's intention to carry out his part of the job. Completion of the task may depend on the agreement or the action of others, and that cannot be rated.

> ◆ **What prevents it from being a 10?** If you have rated yourself at less than eight, how can you reduce the size of the task or lengthen the time scale such that it would enable you to raise the rating to eight or above? If your rating is still below eight, cross out the action step, as you are unlikely to take it.

COMPLETION

This is not to sabotage completion, as it might appear, but it is our experience that those who rate less than eight seldom follow through. However, when faced with having to admit failure, the coachee may all of a sudden find the necessary motivation.

Most of us are familiar with the items that keep recurring on our job lists, be it at work or just the odd jobs around the home. Our list becomes so crumpled and scribbled on that eventually we rewrite it, and those same few items keep getting copied over. In time we begin to feel appropriately guilty but still nothing happens. "How is it that I never complete this?" we moan at ourselves. Our uncompleted job list is evidence of our failure. Well, why feel bad about it? If you aren't going to do something, cross it off your list. And if you want to be a success for ever more, don't put anything on your list that you don't intend to do!

Remember that coaching aims to build and maintain the self-belief of the coachee. We must therefore coach people to success for their own sake as well as for their company.

## CONCLUDING THE COACHING CYCLE

At this point the coaching cycle is complete, but it is up to the coach to hand to the coachee a clear and accurate written record of the action steps agreed and the coachee's answers to all the **will** questions. He should get the coachee to read it and confirm that it is a true record, that it constitutes his plan, that he fully understands it, and that he intends to carry it out. This is when I as coach usually offer myself as further support and reassure the coachee of my accessibility should he need me. Sometimes I offer to initiate the contact myself after a suitable interval just to see how things are going. All this serves to help the coachee realize that he matters. I want the coachee to leave the session feeling good about himself and about his chances of getting the job done. If he does, then it will be achieved.

Let us look at how Mike handles this final and important **will** phase with Joe.

MIKE    Well, Joe, we have a list here. Let me remind you:

Running more often, further or faster.
Eating and drinking less and more healthily.
Visiting a gym.
Swimming.
Squash.
Golf.
Cycling.
Walking.
Running upstairs.
· Weights and/or exercises at home.

Which of these are you going to do?
JOE    I am definitely going to continue running, with a minimum of three times a week for 20 minutes.
MIKE    When are you going to start that?
JOE    Next week, with the first run on Tuesday.
MIKE    Which day and what time each day are you going to run?
JOE    Usually Tuesday and Thursday immediately I get home from work, and on Sunday mornings. Sunday I'll do half an hour.
MIKE    What else are you going to do?
JOE    I'm going to cut out chips and chocolate altogether.
MIKE    What about drink?
JOE    I was hoping you wouldn't ask that one directly! But yes, no more wine and only half a pint of beer a day.
MIKE    How realistic is that? Can you stick to a half-pint if you are with friends?
JOE    Probably not.

MIKE    I have a suggestion.

JOE    What?

MIKE    Three and a half pints a week. If you overdo it one day you just hold off the next one or two to make good.

JOE    Sounds good – much easier to stick to but with the same result.

MIKE    When do you start?

JOE    Sunday.

MIKE    What other exercise?

JOE    I'll arrange for a couple of squash lessons to see if I like it and can get started.

MIKE    When?

JOE    I knew you were going to ask that! I'll call the pro today and have my first lesson next week.

MIKE    And the next lesson?

JOE    The next week.

MIKE    What else?

JOE    Well, I'm certainly not going to start cycling to work in November. I'll put that on the shelf for reconsideration on 1 April.

MIKE    I'll remind you [taking out his diary] and I'm not fooling either!

JOE    Perhaps I could do a few exercises at home meanwhile.

MIKE    What exercises, how often?

JOE    You're the expert, you tell me.

MIKE    We'll come back to that one. Is that it?

JOE    That should be more than enough to meet my goal.

MIKE    I agree, but is it realistic?

JOE    I think so.

MIKE    Now, what obstacles can you foresee?

JOE    Christmas for the food and drink, and extreme weather for the running. That's all. Oh, and my natural laziness.

MIKE    How will you cope with those?

JOE    Give myself an extra couple of pints that week and a plate of chips! I'm on holiday the week after Christmas and I'll do two extra runs.

MIKE    What if there's bad frost or snow then or at any other time?

JOE    I'll replace the running with either squash or a swim. I know what you're going to ask. Forty minutes of squash or twenty lengths of the pool.

MIKE    What about this laziness of yours, which we all have?

JOE    I need a prod every now and again.

MIKE    Just what I was coming to. What support do you need and from whom?

JOE    My wife over the food and to prompt me to run. I'll speak to her about all this tonight.

MIKE    Any other support?

JOE    From you, a phone call every couple of weeks would help, and I'd like you to show me a couple of good exercises at home. I don't want to go and buy weights and all that.

MIKE    Sure, sit-ups like this don't demand someone to hold your feet and are just as good for the stomach muscles. Start with ten and build up your repeats. Squats like this, and push-ups. Again, groups of repetitions are better than forcing. About ten minutes each day would be great.

JOE    Okay, each morning when I get up, and if I miss one day I've got a second chance in the evening. If I miss a whole day, I'll do two stints the following day.

MIKE    When are you going to start this?

JOE    How about tomorrow morning?

MIKE    You've been surprisingly willing to set yourself a fairly ambitious program, given your past history. How would you rate your chances of sticking to it for the next three months on a 1–10 scale?

JOE    That is a tough one – seven, I guess.

MIKE    What part of this could you drop or reduce so you could give yourself a higher rating?

JOE    I think it's just too much, and I'm doubtful about the squash because I won't be able to do that on my own in my own time and at short notice. If I drop that, I'll give myself a nine.

MIKE    Good. One final check, will this regime meet your goal?

JOE    It has altered its emphasis, but I think it exceeds it and I'm very confident I'll succeed.

Not all coaching sessions are as straightforward as this one, and coachees can offer more resistance and complications, but this is fairly typical and it serves to illustrate the majority of the coaching principles.

And as I have said before, most coaching sessions will be less formalized and structured than this one. Most take place in a way that the uninitiated might not even recognize as coaching at all. They would simply think that one person was being particularly helpful and considerate of the other, and was obviously a good listener. Structured or informal, the fundamental principles of raising **awareness** and building **responsibility** within the performer remain the key to good coaching.

# Part II

# The Practice of Coaching

# 11
# What Is Performance?

*If either the quality of a performance or learning from the experience is important, coaching is a must. If neither is, then tell - if you must*

"The execution of the functions required of one" is how my dictionary defines performance, but that sounds not unlike doing the minimum necessary to get by. That is not performance in my view; it is not what I refer to in *Coaching for Performance*.

Real performance is going beyond what is expected; it is setting one's own highest standards, invariably standards that surpass what others demand or expect. It is, of course, an expression of one's potential. This comes closer to the second meaning of performance as defined by my dictionary: "a deed, a feat, a public exhibition of skill." That is what I coach for.

By definition, the full expression of one's potential demands taking total responsibility or ownership. If it did not, it would not be one's own potential, it would be partly someone else's. Coaching is therefore the essential management style or tool for optimizing people's potential and performance. Commanding, demanding, instructing, and persuading with threats, overt or covert, cannot produce sustainable optimum performance, even though they may get the job done.

The question a leader or a manager has to ask himself is how well he wants the job done or how good a performance he is looking for. And does he even know what really good performance would look like? Coaching can lead to performance beyond the expectations of the coach/manager, and beyond the dreams of the performer.

In sport, where success and failure are so clearly defined, the rules are simple, the time span is short, and physical or mental discomfort is determinate, self-motivation is not hard to evoke. The tabloids would have us believe that fame and fortune are the dream of every sports performer. For some, perhaps, but the majority are shooting for less tangible goals such as identity, self-esteem, excellence, and peak experience, uniquely personal rewards only experienced by the recipient.

By comparison, success in business is less glamorous, and slow to come. Quality of life in the workplace, by virtue of the hours and years spent there, takes on far greater importance. Few captains of industry achieve any degree of public recognition and those who do are likely to be more infamous than famous. On the other hand, business offers countless opportunities, both large and small, for personal achievement of goals that can be individually chosen to provide optimal personal growth. Unfortunately, few people manage to view their workplace as a university for self-development, or their chores as challenges. It is hardly surprising, therefore, that their performance lacks sparkle.

We perform quite well on autopilot with our attention elsewhere, but higher performance demands fuller attention and no distractions

## THE JOHNSONVILLE SAUSAGE

Let me tell you a story from a long time ago. I am retaining it in this edition precisely to show how far back enlightened business leaders were doing things that produced great successes, but with which other business leaders of today still have not caught up. What is the glue that sticks so many business leaders to the past, to past practices, to past thinking, to past habits, and to past follies? What does it take for people to change? Is it death and rebirth? Or could it merely be a serious economic meltdown?

The story is of a company with the unlikely name of Johnsonville Sausage. That was the name of a family sausage-making business in Wisconsin, which in 1980 was under the stewardship of Ralph Stayer. Stayer wrote about his company in the November/December 1990 issue of the *Harvard Business Review* under the title "How I learned to let my workers lead," from which I quote here.

Growth, sales, and profits were good at Johnsonville Sausage, giving all the indications of a successful business, but… "What worried me more than the competition… was the gap between potential and performance," wrote Stayer. "No one was deliberately wasting money, time, and materials; it was just that people took no responsibility for their work. They showed up in the morning, did half-heartedly what they were told to do, and then went home."

The situation that Stayer describes is all too common, but he clearly recognized the vital role responsibility plays in bringing performance up to potential. On his own admission, Stayer then "went from authoritarian control to authoritarian abdication." He forced responsibility on his management team and expected them to guess what he wanted. It did not work, though. "The early 1980s taught me that I couldn't give responsibility. People had to expect it, want it, even demand it… To bring people to that… I had to learn to be a better coach."

He changed his approach. The sausage makers started tasting the sausages instead of the top management doing it, and they took charge of quality control and of making improvements to the product and its packaging. Next the shop floor raised the issue of poor-performing colleagues:

*We offered to help them set performance standards and to coach them in confronting poor performers, but we insisted that since they were the production-performance experts it was up to them to deal with the situation. I bit my tongue time and time again, but they took on the responsibility for dealing with performance problems and actually fired individuals who wouldn't perform up to the standards of their teams.*

Before long the Johnsonville workforce was responsible for the vast majority of functions. Terms like employee and subordinate were dropped in favour of "members" of the organization, and managers became known as "coordinators" or "coaches." This change in language set the tone of the renewed organization, in which promotion came from ability as a teacher, coach, and facilitator, rather than from managing or problem solving in the traditional sense.

Stayer noticed that the workforce:

*wanted to see if I practiced what I preached. From the outset I did simple things to demonstrate my sincerity. I made a sign for my desk that said THE QUESTION IS THE ANSWER, and when people came in to me with questions, I asked myself if they were questions I should answer. Invariably they weren't. Invariably people were asking me to make decisions for them. Instead of giving answers, I turned the tables and asked the questions myself, trying to make them repossess their own problems.*

As time went on the "members" were empowered to take strategic decisions, and did so successfully, and Stayer even began to see himself as a consultant to his own company.

*When I began this process of change ten years ago. I looked forward to the time when it would be all over and I could get back to my real job. But I've learned that change is the real job of every effective business leader because change is about the present and the future not about the past. There is no end to change. Yet another thing I've learned is that the cause of excitement at Johnsonville Sausage is not change itself but the process used in producing change. Learning and responsibility are invigorating, and aspirations make our hearts beat.*

*Getting better performance from any group or individual, yourself included, means permanent change in the way you think and run your business. Change of this kind is not a single transaction but a journey, and the journey has a specific starting point [reality] and a clear destination [goal].*

*So to make the changes that will lead to great performance, I recommend focusing on goals, expectations, contexts, actions, and learning.*

Stayer clearly practiced what he preached. The workforce responded with performance that was exceptional, and no doubt learning and enjoyment were very high too at Johnsonville Sausage. How much courage does it take to initiate radical changes in an organization? Any business leader who seeks to be assured of real performance, and perhaps survival in the uncertain future, will need to make big changes. But where does one start?

Coaching for performance improvement in oneself, in others, and in teams is simple and straightforward provided that its underlying principles are fully embraced, and the adoption of a coaching management style is where change begins. However, even managers who use coaching widely may fail if they focus exclusively on performance improvement.

Many businesses are beginning to recognize that they need to become learning organizations if they are going to stimulate and motivate their staff and if they are going to cope with the demand for almost continual change. Performance, learning, and enjoyment are inextricably intertwined. All three are enhanced by high awareness levels, a fundamental objective of coaching, but it is possible to focus primarily on the development of one of them quite successfully, though only for a while. When one of the three is neglected, sooner or later the other two will suffer. For example, performance cannot be sustained where there is no learning or where there is no enjoyment.

Many professional sports performers have experienced periods of losing the enjoyment of their sport. Likewise, the enjoyment of basking on a beach may fade after a day or three and we begin to seek challenges to our performance with paddle tennis or new skills like scuba diving. Schools of learning that do not offer the challenges of the performing arts or sports and that frown on enjoyment are unable to maintain the high standards they so urgently and exclusively seek. The very definition of performance, for coaching purposes, should include learning and enjoyment too.

# 12
# Learning and Enjoyment

*We do not have to know how to do something to be able to do it*
*We learned to walk, run, ride a bike, and catch a ball without instructions*

Much of this book so far has been about learning. The learning of physical skills in sport has provided a number of examples illustrating the coaching process. But the widespread use of instructional methods of teaching in sport, at work, and at school is an indication of how poor general understanding remains about how we really learn. Part of the problem is that instructors, teachers, and managers are concerned more about short-term gain, passing the exam, or getting the job done now than they are about learning or about the quality of performance. This is going to have to change, because results are simply not good enough to meet our needs or to surpass the competition. We have to find a better way.

Participants on our coaching courses are struck by how obvious and commonsensical the principles of coaching are, by their irrefutable logic – once we can escape from the tyranny of old, redundant thinking patterns that we have never thought to doubt or question. Many find helpful a way of looking at learning that is widely accepted in business training circles. It postulates four stages of learning:

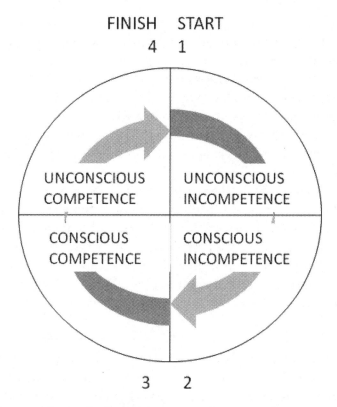

FINISH    START
   4         1

3    2

- **Unconscious incompetence** = low performance, no differentiation or understanding.
- **Conscious incompetence** = low performance, recognition of flaws, and weak areas.
- **Conscious competence** = improved performance, conscious, somewhat contrived effort.
- **Unconscious competence** = natural, integrated, automatic higher performance.

The learning cycle generally takes us through each of these segments in turn. As one piece of learning becomes fully integrated, and if we are endeavoring to continue to improve, we embark on the next cycle.

Do we always have to follow these four stages, or are there exceptions or accelerations? A child learns to walk and talk, throw and catch, run and ride a bicycle by passing fairly directly from **unconscious incompetence** to **unconscious competence**. Later, when a teenager learns to drive a car, the four stages are clearly identifiable, with the driving instructor's input applied in the **conscious incompetence** and **conscious competence** stages. After the driving test, learning continues in **conscious competence** and evolves into **unconscious competence** as the act of driving becomes more integrated. Soon we are able to drive relatively automatically while concentrating on our thoughts, on a conversation, or on the sounds of a CD. Driving skill continues to improve slowly by experience.

Learning can also be accelerated by consciously setting out round the cycle again. This can be done in two ways, either by employing an advanced driving instructor to take us through stages 2 and 3, or by a process of self-coaching. The first way assumes that we are incapable of determining what we are doing wrong and what we should do differently in future. We give responsibility for improvements in our driving to another person.

With the second method we retain that responsibility, shutting off the radio and our extraneous thoughts so we can observe or become aware of different aspects of our driving. If this is done consciously, nonjudgmentally, and honestly, those areas of our driving that need improvement will reveal themselves. It might be harsh gear changes, misjudgment of speed and distance on occasion, or tension in the arms and shoulders causing premature tiredness. We are now in the phase of **conscious incompetence**, and we are likely to enter the next phase by making a conscious effort to operate the clutch more smoothly and watch the rev counter, or watch the speedometer and always leave a set distance between our vehicle and the one in front. Eventually and by conscious repetition, the improvements become a habit and **unconscious competence** commences.

There is, however, a very important variation on this theme of self-coaching that is far more effective. Instead of making the effort to change certain flawed aspects of driving that have been identified in **conscious incompetence**, we can achieve better results with less effort by doing the following.

We identify the quality we would like to bring in, say smoothness in gear changes, and, rather than trying to change gear smoothly, we simply continue to observe how smooth our gear changes are. In order to quantify this to give ourselves more precise feedback measurement, we might create a 1–10 smoothness scale, with 10 representing a gear change that could not be felt at all. We would drive as normal but simply rate the smoothness to ourselves after each gear change. With no increase of effort the numbers will begin to rise, and in a surprisingly short time they are likely to hover between nine and ten.

**Unconscious competence** slips in, monitoring of the scale falls away, and smooth gear changes are maintained even when driving conditions become extreme or we are driving an unfamiliar vehicle. If any lapse does occur, a mere mile or two of **conscious competence** monitoring and rating will restore the smoothness. This effort-free learning or performance improvement is surprisingly fast and delivers a higher-quality result.

In process terms, this is a leap from **conscious incompetence** directly into **unconscious competence** without going through the phase of **conscious competence**. The driving instructor will keep us wallowing in **conscious incompetence** and **conscious competence**, at great expense of time and money. However, he provides the consciousness, such as it is, by his criticisms and his instructions, neither of which are owned by the learner. The more critical and dictatorial he is, the more ownership is undermined.

There is a world of difference between continuously trying to do something right and continuously monitoring what we are doing nonjudgmentally. It is the latter, the input–feedback loop, that results in quality learning and performance improvement – this is allowing rather than forcing. It is the stressful former that is the least effective and the most used in common practice.

## ENJOYMENT

Were I to devote an entire chapter to enjoyment in a book primarily intended for the business reader, it might cause a raised eyebrow or two. It is a subject that deserves its own chapter, but I will restrain myself! Enjoyment is experienced in many different ways by different people, but I will attempt to boil it down to its essence, in a couple of paragraphs.

Enjoyment is primarily experienced through our senses. Due to the comfortable physical security of our modern world, we are less often exposed to extreme sensations by the normal events of life at home or at work, so we invent ever more radical sports and leisure pursuits to activate our feelings. We seek ever steeper, higher, faster, tougher stimulants – but we can enjoy equally strong responses merely by enhancing our senses to experience greater subtlety. As we become more aware of our senses, ordinary, everyday sensations become literally sensational. Daily, common-or-garden events can provide intense enjoyment if we experience them more fully with all our senses.

The senses provide us with the experience of what is happening in our body, our emotions, and our thoughts while it is happening. It is the continuous experience of the "now." In fact all experience happens now; recalling an experience is not the same as the experience itself, it is thinking about the past. Similarly, anticipating an experience is thinking about what it may be like in the future; it distracts from the experience.

Real enjoyment, real pleasure comes from experiencing something as it is happening, not thinking about a past or future experience. In fact, many people often allow their mind to stray ahead of the experience, and thereby lose the experience itself. I make no apology for referring you to the most obvious example, sexual experiences with your partner, because it so clearly illustrates the value of both parties experiencing the now, as opposed to being in the past or the future.

Playing sport is another example of an activity that needs to be experienced in the now, but so many sportspeople spoil

*Focused attention or relaxed concentration describe the same passive receptive state*

their enjoyment by being in the past (what they just failed to do) or the future (fearing what might occur). Not only do they lose the enjoyment, their performance also suffers because quality awareness, the feedback from their own body, is greatly reduced. This is at the core of the Inner Game coaching process derived from sport. Living more of our time in the now is key to a rich quality of life. Even normally mundane activities can be transformed into joy when fully experienced with high awareness. This is a huge subject that I will not pursue further now but, for those who are interested, I recommend a couple of popular books on the subject, *The Power of Now* by Ekhart Tolle and *Presence* by Peter Senge *et al*.

This heightened awareness can be created in a number of ways: by deprivation or devotion, by meditation or medication, by exercise or ecstasy, but also by the simple and risk-free means of self-coaching. Asking ourselves precisely what we feel, touch, hear, see, smell, taste, and even think – focusing to find the answers – heightens our awareness and our enjoyment. It gives us more and better feedback or high-quality relevant input.

Another associated form of enjoyment comes from the experience of a fuller expression of our potential. Each time we experience ourselves stretching to somewhere we have never been before in exertion, in courage, in activity, in fluidity, in dexterity, in effectiveness, we reach new heights in our senses, accentuated by the flow of adrenalin. Coaching works directly on the senses, particularly where physical activities are concerned. Therefore coaching by its very nature enhances enjoyment. In practice, the distinction between performance, learning, and enjoyment becomes blurred, and at the limit of this merger lies what is often described as the peak experience. Far be it from me to be promoting peak experiences at work, but there is a serious side to this: the need to understand the way coaching works, and awareness in particular.

Self-esteem, confidence and performance are seamless. So must be performance, learning and enjoyment – if performance is to be sustained

# 13
# Motivation and Self-Belief

*The carrot and the stick are pervasive and persuasive motivators*
*But if you treat people like donkeys, they will perform like donkeys*

The secret of motivation is the Holy Grail that every business leader would dearly love to find. The carrot and the stick, those symbolic external motivators, are becoming less and less effective. Few managers doubt that self-motivation would be better, but forcing someone to motivate themselves is a contradiction in terms. Self-motivation dwells within the mind of each individual, out of reach of even the chiefest of executives. Motivation would also appear to be easier to come by in sport than it is in business, although many sports people and their coaches are also seeking more of it. What, if anything, can we learn from sport?

The majority of sports involve the body and mind in a skill that demands balance, timing, fluidity, extension, exertion, and strength in different combinations. The closer we come to using our body to the fullness of its unique potential, the more pleasure we experience from the sensations generated. Sport is therefore inherently enjoyable to the extent of being somewhat addictive; mental or physical work is far less so, at least for the majority of people. Clearly, sport has a motivational advantage here. There are other factors too.

The external rewards from sport are more immediate, more glamorous, and, at the top, often richer in fortune and in fame. More importantly, however, sports performances at all levels are ultimately in the hands of the performers (they have total responsibility). Added to that, the choice to take up sport, any sport, in the first place is often driven by a desire for self-worth and identity. This constitutes a large measure of self-motivation – and now we have all the winning ingredients.

Because there is limited inherent enjoyment at work, at least for those who do not experience the responsibility advantage of working for themselves, employers have had to rely on external motivators. We all need money. That money motivates is not in question, but if it comes in the form of minimal increases, toughly negotiated and reluctantly given, it motivates minimally.

## CARROT AND STICK

Ever since work began, people have resorted to a combination of threat and reward to get other people to do what they want. If we go far enough back in history to the time of slavery, it was all stick and no carrot. As time went on, carrots were introduced in the hope that people would perform better, and they did, by a little for a while. So next we tried washing the carrots, cooking them, and providing bigger ones too, and we tried padding the stick or even hiding it, pretending we didn't have one, until we needed it once more. Again performance improved – a little.

At present we are faced with economic constraints on pay increases, unless you are already rich, and there are ever fewer opportunities for promotion. During an economic debacle, an absence of demotion is the best that many can hope for. We are desperate for higher performance and we are running out of carrots. The stick is increasingly being seen as politically incorrect. So the motivation system is failing us, but that's not a moment too soon and besides, it never worked that well anyway. People at work by and large do not perform up to their potential, as a glance at how well they can perform in a real emergency readily shows.

The carrot and stick analogy originates from donkey motivation. In my memory the performance of donkeys is hardly inspiring. I hope I am not doing donkeys an injustice if I say that in fact they will do as little as they can get away with. If we treat people like donkeys, they will perform like donkeys. We must fundamentally change our ideas about motivation. If people are really going to perform, they must be self-motivated.

Research has consistently shown that both job security and the quality of life in the workplace have a high priority for a considerable proportion of people. When either of these internal motivators is absent, money, the most obvious external motivator, takes on a greater significance: "It's the only thing we can get here, so we'll fight for every penny we can get." However, if money is perceived, given, and received as a measure of self-worth, there is a fairly logical explanation for its higher significance.

## MOTIVATION AND MASLOW

In the 1950s an American psychologist, Abraham Maslow, broke the mold of delving into pathology to try to understand human nature. Instead, he studied mature, complete, successful, and fulfilled people, and concluded that we could all be that way. In fact, he asserted that this was the natural human state. All we had to do, in his opinion, was to overcome our inner blocks to development and maturity. Maslow, along with Carl Rogers and others, was the father of the more optimistic wave of psychological thinking that is still in the process of displacing carrot-and-stick behaviorism as the best way of managing and motivating people. Psychological optimism is essential if we are fully to embrace coaching as the management style of the future.

Maslow is best known in business circles for his hierarchy of human needs. This model suggests that our most basic need is for food and water, and that we will care for little else (except possibly a mobile phone!) until that need is met. Once we have secured a supply of food and water, we begin to concern ourselves with items such as shelter, clothing, and safety. Again, when we have met these physical needs, at least

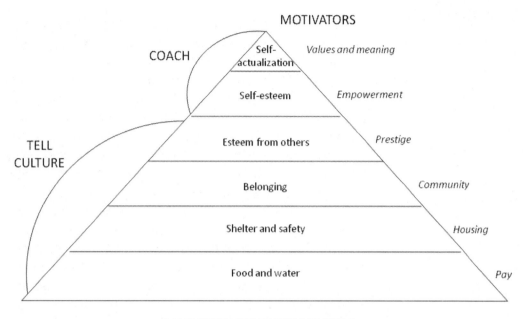

MASLOW'S HIERARCHY OF NEEDS

in part, we begin to focus on our social needs, as Maslow described it the need to belong to a grouping. These needs are met in part by our family, but later we also meet them in pubs, clubs, and teams.

Next we seek to satisfy our desire for the esteem of others, by display and by competing with them for power, victory, or recognition. These needs are emotional ones, but are dependent on the presence of others and are eventually displaced by a subtler esteem need, for self-esteem, or as I prefer to call it self-belief. Here we demand higher standards of ourselves and look to our own criteria by which we measure ourselves, rather than to how others see us.

Maslow's highest state was the self-actualizing person who emerges when both the esteem needs are satisfied and the individual is no longer driven by the need to prove himself, either to himself or to anyone else. These latter two needs are personal and are free of any external dependency. He called this self-actualizing, because self-actualized would have implied that we could really arrive there, whereas he saw it as a never-ending journey. The primary need associated with self-actualizers is the need for meaning and purpose in their lives. They want their work, their activities, and their existence to have some value, to be a contribution to others.

## MOTIVATION AT WORK

How does all this relate to motivation? People will seek to engage in those activities that help them to meet their needs. They are likely to be only partially conscious of this process, because work has naturally developed in ways that do help to meet those needs. However, the more our motivation systems are geared to the levels of needs of those we wish to motivate, the happier everyone is going to be.

Work does meet people's primary needs by giving them an income with which they can feed, water, and clothe their families and pay their housing costs. The staff canteen also helps to take care of those needs, as did tied housing in the past. Work brings people together into a work community. Furthermore, work offers promotion, prestige, pay grades, and even a company car in which to solicit the esteem of others. The normal motivator used in work, rewards in various currencies, goes some of the way to meeting the survival needs, the belonging needs, and even the lower of the two esteem needs. Very clever so far.

A glance into history will reveal that a few decades ago there was a far greater emphasis on tied housing and work social and sports clubs than there is now, and far less on promotion and prestige. In other words, society today is collectively seeking need satisfaction slightly higher up the hierarchy. Reward systems are beginning to reflect the changes at that level.

The need toward which a large segment of modern society is beginning to move is self-belief. Traditional businesses and management methods are very poor at meeting this need. In fact, managers fail to do so principally because their desire to feel in control discourages them from building self-belief in those they manage.

From time to time economic downturns, downsizing, job insecurity, minimal pay increases, and declining house prices lead large numbers of workers to fall back down the hierarchy. When this occurs, the spectrum of predominant needs in society becomes broader. Worse still, many businesses can no longer easily supply those things that attract the esteem of others, such as promotion and company cars. So how will businesses motivate their people? They must continue to meet the basic needs while making the fundamental changes necessary to enable them to meet employees' emerging higher needs.

SELF-BELIEF

Whereas Maslow used the collective term esteem needs and made the important distinction between esteem from others and self-esteem, I prefer to use more descriptive terms, for the former status and recognition, and for the latter self-belief.

Self-belief is not met by prestige and privilege, which are more symbolic than substantial. It is built when someone is seen to be worthy of making choices. Promotion without genuine empowerment and the opportunity to express potential is counterproductive. While telling negates choice, disempowers, limits potential, and demotivates, coaching does the opposite.

CORPORATE VALUES AND THE FUTURE

Some employees, especially younger ones, are showing signs of seeking self-actualizing needs. They want their work to be of value and to have meaning and purpose. Lining the pockets of shareholders is no longer seen as meaningful. Companies are being obliged to consider more carefully their ethics and values and the needs of all their stakeholders, employees, customers, the community, and the environment.

This issue is being raised more and more frequently by staff and managers on the courses we run. Companies are seeking a change of management style, but employees are demanding it. If these young and, in Maslow's terms, more mature employees are not to become disaffected, the changes will have to get underway soon. They will inevitably take time, and there is not much time left. So little time, in fact, and so important is this issue that in this edition I have added several chapters that address it more fully. Work on values is becoming a key realm for coaches and it demands a deeper level of understanding.

## THE CHOICE OF MANAGEMENT BEHAVIOR

*Self-belief is the lifeblood of performance at work*

Of the four criteria that cause us to adopt our management behavior in the moment, the development of our staff gets the lowest priority. At the head of the list comes time pressure, then fear, next comes the quality of the job or the product, leaving staff development a poor fourth. Shortage of time and excess fear drive us into command and control, while the quality of work and the need for development demand coaching.

It comes as little surprise that coaching is sometimes sidelined by short-termism and the urgency of the need to provide shareholder returns. However, the wake-up call has been sounded and that is the changing expectations of younger staff. At job interviews they want to know what training and development opportunities and what management style they can expect. They do not seek – nor do they want – a job for life, and they will leave a job if their needs are not met. And those needs are for things that will help their self-belief, such as a coaching management style.

This notion is further supported by the recognition that many bright young staff have already reached the self-belief level, while the majority of our postindustrial western society is still in the status and recognition phase, and that includes many executives. There are two problems with this. One is that bosses assume that their staff are either in the same stage or below them in the hierarchy, and therefore do not recognize the importance of self-belief for their workers. The other is that some young managers lose respect for bosses who appear to be less psychologically evolved than themselves. The executives' need for status and their command-and-control behavior become the butt of jokes or scorn.

Self-belief is a very useful yardstick against which to assess the impact of our behavior on others. It is far easier, if more painful, to look at our interventions with others in terms of how they enhance or damage another's self-belief. All instruction, all criticism, every reduction in choice, every manifestation of hierarchy, every act of secrecy subtly lowers people's self-belief. Coaching, trust, openness, respect, authentic praise, freedom of choice, and, of course, success raise it.

## MASLOW AND LEADERSHIP

Part III deals with leadership for high performance, but I will illustrate in more depth here how leadership can be viewed through the Maslow prism.

Aside from an obvious and common desire for the esteem of others and a sense of self-importance, many people who want to lead do not know *why* they want to lead. I assert that what makes a good leader depends more on the "What for?" than on the "How to." By way of illustrating this, since basic needs come first, if you are thirsty and you lead your family to a stream it would seem to be an entirely benevolent act. However, did you ascertain that they were thirsty too before setting out? Were you really the best-equipped person to lead, or might your younger brother have been more familiar with the route? Did you want the approval of your parents or the admiration of the younger ones?

Might your mother, who also knew the route, have been a better choice of leader since she would understand more about the most appropriate pace for the weaker members of the family? Did you consult your wise old grandfather who knew the vagaries of the weather and the habits of dangerous animals better than anyone? Did your need to exercise your masculinity push you to take the lead role? Was it not an opportunity to boost your sibling's confidence by encouraging him or her to lead the way? Did you lead because you felt you were the best person to fend off any wild animal that you happened across, or was it because you wanted to present yourself as a hero should that happen? Was it the dark secret that you wanted to be safely in front since a marauding pack of wolves tends to pick on the weakest one at the back?

So leading the proverbial horse to water can appear to be an entirely benevolent act, but at any time a combination of other driving forces is in play. Could the journey have had multiple other side benefits as well, if other factors were taken into account? And don't forget that consultation before setting out, not only with the grandfather but with the whole family. Perhaps the ideal solution might have been to have your younger brother leading with your mother just behind in charge of regulating the pace and you in the middle to respond to any attack. If so, that would have been good leadership. How would you have fared given this example?

## STATUS AND RECOGNITION

I suspect that when our culture was at the level of basic need there was far less game playing and inappropriate leadership than there is today. We want to be accepted and liked, so we adopt strategies and behaviors that will give us that result. For example, leaders who are primarily motivated by this personal need seek to be seen as a nice leader, humble enough to be liked but strong enough to carry another's responsibility. They will seek popularity and therefore not push the envelope, or their people. But beware, more than one nice leader has a hired gun behind him and together they operate the sinister and manipulative good cop, bad cop game. Working under a genuinely nice leader is comfortable, not very taxing, pretty secure, and he or she pays attention to team working. However, achievement and change might be slow in coming.

This sounds all very cosy, but watch out if this leader begins to move up into the level of status and recognition. He, because it generally will be a he, is likely to become uncharacteristically assertive and demanding and expect progress and results that he cared little about before. His clothing will get sharper and he will probably acquire a new car, a deluxe model. He is now in a role on a roll, and will probably get worse. You should consider jumping ship, because even if in the past you saw him as something of an equal, you never will again and he is a whole lot less likely to join you in the pub for a pint. All this occurs independent of any acquired leadership skills, emotional intelligence, or general knowledge; or the absence of them.

The problem is that none of us occupies one of Maslow's levels at a time; we move between several according to varying external and internal factors. The complex mix of subpersonalities of which we are made up (more on this in Chapter 24) may occupy several different levels and therefore sometimes be in conflict with each other. That is hard enough for us to cope with, but it is even harder for others, who thus find us unpredictable. To make it more difficult still, much of this goes on at a subconscious level and the perpetrator does not fully know what he is doing or why he is doing it.

Most business leaders today have reached Maslow's status and recognition level and this is where leaders can do the most harm. They are often arrogant, assertive, domineering, and self-important. They will do anything to get more pay, even though they don't need or deserve it, but it is a way of measuring and asserting their status.

However, if a business leader does escape the trap and progress to the next level, the need for self-belief, the leadership news gets better. Leaders who aspire to be there, or are there, will really try to do the "right" thing, rather than trying to appear to do the right thing or to do the thing right. Only being authentic gives the feel-good factor that accompanies self-belief. What this is all about, of course, is the emergence of broader altruistic values – of leading for others rather than for oneself.

Leadership by a leader any lower than this on the scale has a selfish element regardless of the other skills he might possess. Such leadership is only useful to those he leads if they happen to have the same aspirations. And while a leader at the level of self-belief is well motivated, he might seek to be a little more high profile than a leader who has reached the next level – self-actualizing. This is sometimes called the level of service. Service is often seen as the answer to the search for meaning and purpose, something that people used to gain from their religion but now look for elsewhere, including while at work. Service to others manifests in a wide spectrum of forms, is very fulfilling, and is the universal way to meeting this need.

Toward the end of his life Maslow added another level that he called self-realization. However, as I have said, development is a journey, not a destination. Some recent commentators also define self-actualizing more modestly and flatter business leaders by suggesting that they, and indeed many others, are at this level. I do not share that view. As far as I am concerned, in order to earn the title leader a person must have evolved beyond the status and recognition level and beyond self-interest. Aspiring leaders will hone their leadership skills at lower levels while they are growing into the job, but their power to exercise control over others should be constrained until they have grown up.

Of course, most young people want to prove themselves to others at some stage (status and recognition) of their developmental journey. In a crisis, war, or disaster they might be obliged to lead anyway, but interestingly enough, younger people forced into such positions often rise to the occasion and experience a temporary or even more permanent leap up Maslow's ladder. In practice, our level on the ladder has little to do with age, and increasingly younger people in the workplace are displaying levels of maturity beyond their years and beyond their superiors, creating an inversion in maturity – and in respect – in the office.

The problem occurs when an older person, for whatever reason, acquires power, and people to exercise it over, before he has reached the level of self-belief. Many senior business people have remained stuck in status and recognition for decades, and may never get beyond it. Far too many immature older people exercise vast power with self-interest, acquisition, and possession as their main objectives, while managing to conceal it with nice words, and they control the lives of billions. This has never been better illustrated than by Freddie Mac and Fannie Mae, barmy bankers, tricky traders, private equity prats, hedge fund fools, and derivative dolts, along with pathetic politicians that led us into the economic crisis – but while we curse them, let us not forget that it was our own greed, ignorance, and lack of self-responsibility that allowed them to lead us to the slaughter.

The good news is that change is in the air, evolution marches on despite expected resistance, corporate social responsibility is gaining traction, and consumer and public demand for transparency is becoming more effective at policing business excesses, often via the internet. Hopefully new government controls will shackle the wayward bankers, though at the time of writing they are not making much headway in the pay and bonus stakes. It is people's status and recognition need that causes them to demand vast sums in salary and bonuses; they don't really need the money. Guilt then makes a few give some of it away to a social cause – or is that another chance to collect accolades, a second bite of the recognition cherry? Of course the worthy cause benefits and that is welcome, so you may say it is churlish to criticize them, but they could certainly use a good coach and some self-development and feedback.

# 14
# Coaching for Meaning and Purpose

*Man's search for meaning is the primary motivation in his life and not a secondary rationalization of instinctual drives. (Viktor Frankl,* Man's Search for Meaning, *1959)*

I mentioned in Chapter 13 that self-actualizers seek meaning and purpose and very often find it by contributing to others, to their community, or to society at large. More and more people are demonstrating that they care as much about fairness and the plight of others as they do about themselves. These emerging altruistic tendencies are also causing them to question corporate ethics and values as well as the profit motive. It is not surprising, therefore, that global investment in what are called ethical funds is increasing fast, that sexism and racism, previously endemic in many workplaces, are now widely condemned, and that corporate social responsibility and triple bottom-line reporting are increasingly adopted.

The drive for these changes is coming from ordinary people who want more say in how they are treated at work and by business. However, climate change is also sending all of us, and business in particular, some harsh messages about our values, behaviors, and responsibilities in the global context. In addition, the potential consequences of the intensive farming of animals, of biofuels and genetic modification of crops are forcing serious re-evaluation of agricultural methods that is way beyond the province of mere "nature lovers." What will the next beachhead be? It will certainly be in the sustainability arena, but we don't know where it will come from as nature's system controls are breaking down, and we are now past the point at which her reactions are predictable. The next point is the one of no return. It is all far more serious than is suggested by short-term and wholly inadequate political and corporate responses.

With all this going on, it is not surprising that the issue of meaning and purpose is being raised more and more often on coach training programs, stemming from the desire to escape from what many see as the meaningless corporate world and to go independent. On the other hand, coaching is an invaluable tool in this environment for helping staff clarify their own thoughts, since as long as they remain confused and frustrated they are unlikely to give of their best. Countered by their need for security, some people may well choose to stay put for a time, but dissatisfaction is likely to haunt them. Others may leave the organization anyway, but most can discover how to find meaning in their existing work, or in part-time charity or community activities outside work, and thereby maintain their performance with greater willingness and satisfaction.

Meaning and purpose are spoken of as being joined at the hip, but they are not identical and they need to be distinguished. Meaning is the significance we ascribe to an event or an action in hindsight, while purpose is our intent to embark on a course of action. Meaning is mainly psychological, whereas purpose is a spiritual concept. To be more precise, we should specify either meaning, or purpose, or both.

MEANING AND PURPOSE – THE DIFFERENCE

## COACHING QUESTIONS FOR MEANING AND PURPOSE

I list below the sort of coaching questions I use with these issues, always bearing in mind that in practice, my next question will invariably be determined by the answer I received from the previous one. I am assuming that the coachee in this case has already indicated that he wishes to work on improving the quality of his work life. I always try to start positively and with the coachee's goal – the ideal for him:

GOAL

- What would you like to have by the end of this coaching session?
- Let's imagine a year or so into the future. What would your ideal work situation be? Describe to me in some detail what your typical working day would be like. (This may be in or out of his current job, with no judgment on my part.)
- What are the elements of that scenario that you yearn for most at this time?
- How important is each of these to you? (You could use a 1–10 scale.)
- So your goal at work would be what?
- By when would you want that to be the case?
- Deep down, what do you really want from your work life?
- If that seems a bit of a stretch from where you are now, give me a couple of stepping stones along the way.
- From where you are now, what would be a first step that you could feel good about?

REALITY

- How much of this situation do you feel is within your control? (Frequently it is a big issue for coachees to realize that ultimately their situation is their choice. They so often feel a victim and therefore experience themselves as powerless.)
- Aside from the day-to-day frustrations, what is it about your work that gives you the most dissatisfaction?
- What is the concern that lies behind the dissatisfaction?
- What sort of thing could meet that concern?
- What else bothers you? And what else? Tell me more about that.
- What sort of people and what sort of activities at work do you dislike?
- For how much of your time at work do you feel positive and how much negative? Let's look at the positive.

- What sort of people and activities do you enjoy most at work?
- What is it about those people and those activities that you like?
- What qualities do they represent? Where else do you find those qualities?
- What activities in or out of work are meaningful to you?
- If you had to state a purpose for your life, what would it be?
- If you had the opportunity to write your obituary now, what would you like to be writing about your life? (A good one, but be careful who you use it with!)

<br>

- What options do you have for changing things? (If the coachee answers "I could change my job," continue as follows but bear in mind that changing forms and structures does not change anything. It is consciousness that must change.)
- What would be the benefits of doing that? What would you lose?
- How might you ensure that the same problems would not arise in a new job?
- What sort of job? How would you find it? How secure would that be?
- So changing jobs and going independent are two options. Let's now look at how you might introduce some of those qualities you seek into your current work.
- How else? Where? And where else?
- What would have to change? What could you do to change that? Who could you ask to have other parts changed?
- If you were able to change all those things, how well would your needs be met?

OPTIONS

This is by no means an exhaustive set of questions, but I hope it does provide a line of questioning that you might usefully pursue in sessions of this nature. The above are intentionally not all phrased as questions in order to illustrate a way of avoiding the inquisitorial effect of every sentence ending with a question mark.

WILL

Eventually we would get to a set of will questions to tie the coachee down to real action, either within the current job or elsewhere, but without the coach's influence or prejudice either way. We always have to remember that the coachee's self-belief is paramount, so succeeding and making his own choices about how to do so are also paramount.

# 15

# Feedback and Assessment

*The worst feedback is personal and judgmental*
*The most effective is subjective and descriptive*

So far we have considered coaching as a tool for addressing existing issues of planning, problem solving, reviewing, skill development, and the like, and we have considered motivation. In this chapter I am going to demonstrate a way of using coaching for giving feedback, and for self and team assessment and development.

## FEEDBACK

We can identify five levels of feedback that are in common use. They are illustrated below in order from A, the least helpful, to E, the most productive and the only one of the five that promotes major learning and performance benefits. The other four at best produce minimal short-term improvement, and at worst cause further decline in performance and self-esteem. The first four are widely used in business circles and at first glance seem reasonable – that is, until or unless they are examined with care.

A. Manager's exclamation: *"You are useless."*
This is a **personalized criticism** that devastates self-esteem and confidence and is bound to make future performance even worse. It contains nothing helpful.

B. Manager's intervention: *"This report is useless."*
This **judgmental comment** directed at the report, not at the person, also damages the performer's self-esteem, though less badly, but it still provides no information on which the writer can act to correct it.

C. Manager's intervention: *"The content of your report was clear and concise, but the layout and presentation were too down-market for its target readership."*
This avoids criticism and provides the performer with **some information** on which to act, but in insufficient detail and it **generates no ownership**.

D. Manager's intervention: *"How do you feel about the report?"*
**The performer now has ownership**, but is likely to give a nonresponse such as "Fine," or to make a **value judgment** of the work such as "Great" or "Lousy," rather than a more useful description.

E. Manager's interventions: *"What is the essential purpose of your report?" "To what extent do you think this draft achieves that?" "What are the other points you feel need to be emphasized?" "Who do you see as the target reader?"* etc.
In response to a series of questions such as these, **the performer/learner gives a detailed, nonjudgmental description** of the report and the thinking behind it.

So why does the form of feedback illustrated in E dramatically accelerate learning and improve performance? Only E meets all the best coaching criteria. In order to answer the manager's questions in E, the performer/learner is compelled to engage his brain and get involved. He has to recollect and formulate his thoughts before he can articulate his responses. This is **awareness**. It helps him to learn how to evaluate his own work and thereby become more self-reliant. This way he "owns" his performance and his assessment of it. This is **responsibility**. When these two factors are optimized, learning occurs. Conversely, if the manager just tells the performer his own opinion, the actual engagement of the performer's brain is likely to be minimal; there is no ownership and no means for the manager to measure what has been assimilated.

The use of descriptive rather than judgmental terminology, either by the performer, as seen in E, or by the manager, as in C, avoids evoking the performer's defensiveness. Defensiveness must be avoided because when it is present, the truth/reality becomes smothered in inaccurate excuses and justifications, which may even be believed by both the performer and the manager and which are no basis for performance improvement. However, in intervention C, as well as in A and B, the manager retains ownership of both the evaluation and the correction, so learning for the future is correspondingly minimized. It can be seen that interventions A–D all fall short of the ideal; nevertheless, they are the ones most frequently used in business.

FEEDBACK

Feedback from ourselves and from others is vital for learning and performance improvement. That feedback needs to cover both the results of the action and the action process itself. For example, where the golf ball lands is the result and the golf swing is the process. The result is easy to determine in sport, but perhaps less easy to measure in business at times. Even in sport, we all too often judge the result of an action, evoking defensive blindness. What we need is the very opposite, an accurate, detailed description of the result. "The ball was out" is more helpful than "You blew that one"; better still is "It was six inches beyond the baseline." We can learn as much from those actions that produce the wrong result as we can from those that give the right one. This feedback can be provided by the coach or the coachee, the latter being by far the best.

Let's now look at process feedback. A tennis coach may observe a student's forehand swing and comment critically, or preferably descriptively, on what he observes. The feedback he offers is founded on the disparity between what he observes and an ideal usually based on his knowledge of the correct way, or on his own way. The observable forehand swing is only the symptom or outward manifestation of a complex array of converging physical and psychological factors that comprise the cause. Any changes to that forehand demanded by the coach will be applied initially at the symptomatic level. Real, lasting change must reach the causal level, better still must be initiated there. The coach is unable to observe the causal level, which resides inside the student whose own high-quality internal feedback is what is ideally required. The student can access this level by raising his physiological and psychological self-awareness. The coaching questions that cause him to do this will only be effective if they follow the feedback principles, which are identical to those used for causing someone to watch the ball.

## FEEDFORWARD

Feedback relates to the past: the immediate past, for example when coaching in real time for sport, or the longer-term past, which will generally be the case in business. It is, however, the anticipation of the question that causes you to be aware in the present, and it is that immediate awareness that produces physiological efficiency. For example, I can say to a student "On the next ball I am going to ask you which part of the movement feels the least comfortable to you." He will be paying attention to his body while he is making the movement, and as a result the inefficiency may well not occur on the very first occasion. I am equating comfort here with biomechanical efficiency, and more obvious perhaps is the fact that any biomechanical inefficiency will be experienced as discomfort in that area.

This is taking us very close to feedforward, or planning in more common parlance. The feedback principles on the previous pages remain true. Those principles are maintained if you are coaching me and I am compelled to describe to you, and therefore to myself, in detail what I am going to do. They are not if you tell me what to do, or even if you ask me whether I know what I am going to do. The quality of the questions determines the quality of the feedforward or planning.

"Who will take this one on?" "How confident are you that you can complete this on time?" "Which element of this are you unsure of?" "What might the obstacles be to achieving this?" "When can you have it done by?" All these questions generate responsibility and ownership, but they also raise awareness of other factors.

Why, then, do we persist in employing the least effective means of feedback? Because we look at it from our point of view, rather than that of the performer; because we say what we want, without understanding the effects of what we say. Whether that stems from habit, poor role models, hierarchical arrogance, or just unthinkingly failing to look beneath the surface will vary from manager to manager. What is important, if we truly wish to bring the best out of people – ourselves, our staff, or even our children – is to rethink and refocus at a fundamental level. Our primary objective must be to understand what the performer/learner needs in order to perform the task well, and to ask, say, or do whatever it takes to help him meet that need. Our own wish to be in control or to display our superior knowledge, or simply our laziness to give up old habits and change, will need to be set aside if we want him to perform. It is hard to break the prevailing mold of behavior, but break it we must.

HARD TO CHANGE

Let's return to our simplest example, watching the tennis ball. It is very important for a tennis player to watch the ball. There is nothing wrong with that. However, *telling* him to do it does not *cause* him to do it. On the other hand, and here is the paradox, the number of times the ball revolves is totally unimportant, but if you ask him to try to count them he will watch the ball in order to count them. Counting the revolutions is only one of many alternative questions, the choice of which depends on the effect being sought.

Consider another example. A tennis player is alternating between hitting the ball long and into the net. The player can only see her efforts in terms of good and bad, success and failure. She judges herself harshly. Self-esteem, confidence, and performance all suffer, as does the quality of her feedback, perhaps made even worse by her turning away in frustration as soon as she knows she has muffed another shot. She tries too hard to correct herself, resulting in struggle, stress, and a tendency to overcompensate, leading to further failure.

Most tennis coaches will attempt to deal with this by a technical "correction" – but they are missing the point. They are tackling the symptom, not the cause. By far the most frequent cause of erratic shots is poor feedback, either about where the ball is coming from or where it is going to. Assuming the latter in this case, the question a wiser coach might ask is: "How high over the net did that ball go?" The coach could have the player call out how high over the top of the net in centimeters the ball goes each time. Getting accurate feedback from the result of her action causes automatic self-correction without effort or strife. Letting go of trying to force the correction (the focus is now on the accuracy of the observation) allows the correction to take place effortlessly and subconsciously. The player's total ownership of the correction is maintained. Of course, the exact height in centimeters by which the ball passes over the net is irrelevant, but the player's focus on and mental recording of the results of her actions are highly relevant.

**Generating high-quality relevant feedback, as far as possible from within rather than from experts, is essential for continuous improvement, at work, in sport, and in all aspects of life.**

## PRAISE

Praise is another form of feedback. It tends to be sparingly offered and hungrily received in the workplace, where criticism abounds. In this context, any increase in positive and reduction in negative feedback would seem desirable.

When there is not enough of something it seems churlish to cast doubt on its value, but a caution is in order. Praise insincerely or gratuitously given is hollow indeed and does more harm than good, for phoneyness and manipulation are far more readily recognized than the perpetrators realize. They cheapen the perpetrator and damage relationships and trust. Even authentic praise can cause difficulty. The person being praised may surrender their ability and willingness to self-assess to the giver of praise, and thereby increase their dependence on the opinions of others. We need to do the opposite, to build the autonomy and self-reliance of our staff.

**Praise must simultaneously be generous, genuine, and judicious.**

STRENGTHS AND WEAKNESSES

In business speak we hear a lot about identifying the strengths and weaknesses of people, of processes, and of products. We can list the strengths and weaknesses of each of these and indeed of ourselves. We can list other things too, such as the qualities required of a prospective employee, the qualities we would like to foster in a work team, or the qualities we would like to develop in ourselves. We can list the functions of our organization, a department, or an individual. We can list the technical skills, interpersonal skills, or manual skills required. Breaking things down into more detail like this is one level of awareness raising.

We can use this list to take awareness raising a step further if we then rate these strengths, weaknesses, qualities, functions, or skills on our now familiar 1–10 scale, either in terms of what we would like them to be, or in terms of what we think they are now.

APPRAISALS

Appraisal systems are common, unpopular, misused, limiting, and yet necessary. In a learning, no-blame culture, they can be very beneficial to all concerned. But when they categorize only past performance and not future potential, or are judgmental and not descriptive, they are beneficial to no one. Circumstances and company objectives and history are so varied that I would not attempt to suggest any universal appraisal system. However, such a system cannot be far wrong if it is in tune with the principles of feedback above, and the principles of self-assessment that follow.

## SELF-ASSESSMENT

A great deal of importance is attached in business to assessing others – peers, subordinates, or even bosses – but *self-assessment* is, in my opinion, the most productive form of assessment. Ratings on skills and qualities given by and to others are best regarded as feedback, valuable stuff on which we can choose to act, rather than as a judgment or the truth, which may have a disempowering impact on us. A video, on the other hand, does show the reality of what happened on that one occasion, but should be used for giving information to a person rather than criticizing them. Self-assessment bypasses the negative effects of criticism and maintains responsibility where it needs to be for effective action and self-improvement. Let me give an example.

QUALITIES

I could list the qualities and skills I would most need to do my job well in random order of importance as the following. In the first column opposite each I could write how I rate myself, and in the second column I could write the rating to which I could reasonably hope to develop myself.

|  | As I am now | Target |
| --- | --- | --- |
| Communicative | 8 | 9 |
| Empathetic | 6 | 9 |
| Patient | 7 | 9 |
| Computer literate | 4 | 7 |
| Administratively capable | 6 | 8 |
| Enthusiastic | 8 | 8 |
| Alert and observant | 8 | 9 |
| Competent in bookkeeping | 5 | 7 |

In doing this I have certainly raised my self-awareness, but in terms of the coaching process I have done more than that.

The first column represents the **reality** and the second a realistic, specific, measurable, positively stated, challenging **goal**. All I need to do is to select which one I want to work on and put in a time frame, and I will have completed the first two stages of a simple self-coaching process.

I need to take some time to list all the **options** I have for developing my chosen skill or quality. If I have selected a quality, I might want to list the positive behaviors associated with people who have an abundance of that quality. The reason for this is that action steps usually take the form of new behaviors, rather than new qualities that take longer to develop. In time it is the success of these new behaviors that will enable me to rate myself more highly in terms of the underlying quality.

Finally, I will ask myself the **will** questions and present myself with an action plan.

## TEAM ASSESSMENT

Variations of this exercise can be used on oneself, on individuals, and with teams. It is particularly interesting to have team members list desirable team qualities and then rate their team on each. The disparity between the figures offers opportunities to discuss the different criteria by which people judge and the different experiences that various members have of the same team.

For example, a team of five were asked to list the four most important team qualities in their eyes. Their lists turned out as follows:

| JOE | MIKE | SUSAN | VALERIE | DAVID |
|---|---|---|---|---|
| Humor | Trust | Support | Cooperation | Tolerance |
| Patience | Courage | Flexibility | Trust | Cohesion |
| Support | Cooperation | Enthusiasm | Compatibility | Trust |
| Friendship | Adaptability | Unselfishness | Support | Commitment |

From these lists a merged list was formed. Cooperation and cohesion were considered to be the same, as were adaptability and flexibility. Each of the team members was asked to rate the team on each quality. They were asked to do this individually on paper before the figures were brought to the flip chart, so that no member's figures were influenced by the figures of others. The result was as follows:

|  | JOE | MIKE | SUSAN | VALERIE | DAVID | Average |
|---|---|---|---|---|---|---|
| Support | 7 | 8 | 4 | 6 | 6 | 6.2 |
| Cooperation | 8 | 7 | 8 | 6 | 9 | 7.6 |
| Trust | 7 | 5 | 5 | 7 | 5 | 5.8 |
| Adaptability | 9 | 7 | 8 | 9 | 6 | 7.8 |
| Patience | 7 | 8 | 4 | 6 | 8 | 6.6 |
| Friendship | 9 | 9 | 7 | 5 | 4 | 6.8 |
| Commitment | 8 | 8 | 9 | 8 | 8 | 8.2 |
| Courage | 5 | 6 | 7 | 7 | 8 | 6.6 |
| Humor | 8 | 6 | 3 | 4 | 5 | 5.2 |
| Enthusiasm | 7 | 7 | 8 | 6 | 7 | 7.0 |
| Compatibility | 6 | 6 | 6 | 7 | 6 | 6.2 |
| Unselfishness | 8 | 7 | 6 | 8 | 6 | 7.0 |
| Tolerance | 7 | 6 | 6 | 6 | 5 | 6.0 |

In this case they were not asked to add to the above ratings a highly personal figure, their rating of how much of each of these qualities they personally contribute to the party. Nor were they asked to rate each other's contribution to the sum total of these qualities in the team. Ratings of this kind can open up huge discussions, disputes, love affairs, and several cans of worms, but if I were to work with a team that was going for gold or on whom my life depended, I would want to do this and more!

What the above figures do show is that trust is an issue that needs to be worked on, that Joe's brand of humor is not much appreciated, particularly by the women, that at times Susan feels got at, and that David feels isolated. There is plenty of scope for individual coaching here, by a peer or by an outside facilitator, and for a team discussion of **options** and a team agreement of what action steps they **will** take to raise the level of several of these qualities.

Coaching to build qualities in teams or individuals is a way of positively framing weaknesses and is far more creative and likely to achieve success than attempting to exorcise the weakness. This is further reinforcement of the desirability of putting **goal** setting ahead of **reality** in the coaching sequence. There are an infinite number of variations of coaching exercises that can be devised out of this basic model, and examples to suit all kinds of situations. Over to you!

REFRAMING
WEAKNESSES

Coaching offers personal control. A primary cause of stress in the workplace is a lack of personal control

# 16
# The Development of a Team

*A small number of people with complementary skills committed to a common purpose, performance goals and ways of working together for which they hold themselves mutually accountable. (Katzenbach & Smith, The Wisdom of Teams)*

We have begun to explore ways of coaching a team to improve its performance, but we need to understand some of the dynamics of team development if we are to get the best out of its members. I use a simple three-stage model that is easy to understand and where each stage is readily recognized in most sports and workplace teams. More complex and sophisticated models exist, but they are of less practical use, in my experience. For the purposes of this model the number of team members can range from a handful to a nationful. Teams of more than 15 or 20 members are likely to be made up of sub-teams, but whether it is a first team or a sub-sub-sub-team, certain characteristics remain the same.

## HIGH-PERFORMING TEAMS

The model I use blends well with the team-qualities exercise in the previous chapter. Using the views of those team members, for example, we could safely say that an effective, high-performing team would be well endowed with:

| | |
|---|---|
| Support | Cooperation |
| Trust | Adaptability |
| Patience | Friendship |
| Commitment | Courage |
| Humor | Enthusiasm |
| Compatibility | Unselfishness |

A team that could reasonably be rated at 10 on each of these qualities would indeed be a high-performing team, and an exceptional one. So how can one get a team into such a state? Some people would say with the right chemistry and a lot of luck. Others might not be so convinced that it would be such a great team, because they believe that some internal friction and competition generate good performance. They believe that, but only because they have never seen anything better. However rare they may be, both in business and in sport, such teams can and do exist.

## STAGES OF TEAM DEVELOPMENT

The first task of a team leader is to understand fully the stages through which a team will develop in order that he may encourage and accelerate the process. A model of team development that people easily understand is now known as Firo B. It is worth revealing its humble origins. Dr. Will Schutz was one of the forerunners of encounter group therapy based at the Esalen Institute in Big Sur, California, along with other legends like Maslow, Perls, and Rogers, the fathers of humanistic psychology. He called his method Firo B after the seminar room that he most often used at Esalen; it was a little larger than the other one in the building, known as Firo A. I was at Esalen at the time in 1970 and I participated in many groups in Firo B. Later I produced and co-directed a feature film at Esalen entitled *Here Comes Every Body*, featuring Will Schutz leading an encounter group.

Group therapy participants find it hard to expose their emotional vulnerabilities until they can feel safe with the other participants, so it is incumbent on the group leader to create that safe environment as fast as possible. Will achieved that by following the principles of his model. It remains the most relevant, simple, and accessible of all the team development models. Will first called the ideal team state the affection stage, however some business people balk at too much affection, so I call it the cooperation stage.

How then do we characterize the two stages through which the team has to pass before it reaches the exalted stage of cooperation, if it ever does?

INCLUSION

The first stage is called **inclusion**, for it is here that people determine if they are, and if they feel they are, a group or a team member. Anxiety and introversion are common, but they may be disguised by compensatory opposite behavior in some people. The need for acceptance and the fear of rejection are strong. Perhaps your parents moved house when you were a child and you suddenly found yourself plunged into a new school of strangers in mid-term. You will recall the feelings well: the feeling of separateness and the need, the desperation to find a friend, just one friend, to feel included, to be like the others and to be liked. Team members may not be very mentally productive in this phase, for their focus will be on their own emotional needs and concerns.

If there is a designated group leader, the members will look to him for acceptance and guidance. They want to conform; they seek to comply. The tone and the example that the leader set at this stage are important because it will quickly become the group's accepted norm. For example, if the leader displays openness and honesty and discloses feelings or even a weakness of his own, others will tend to follow suit and a good relating practice will be established. It is a time of tentativeness, and a good leader will attempt to address and satisfy individual concerns so that the group as a whole can move forward.

Fortunately, for many people this phase does not last too long, although for a few it may take weeks or months to feel part of the team. Those who had a childhood in which they developed a strong sense of personal security – and those who rise to leadership positions tend to be this type – would do well to be tolerant and supportive of those who were not so lucky.

Once the majority of the group feels included, another dynamic emerges, that of individual **assertion**, the name of the middle stage. It is a time of expressing power and of extending boundaries. Animals do this: they mark out their territory (the males, of course) and woe betide any opponent who dares to enter. It is the phase in which the pecking order gets worked out. The polite business term for it is the establishment of roles and functions, but the words are often nicer than the actions. Competition within the team is hot, which may lead to exceptional individual performance, but sometimes at the expense of others. It is a phase in which people try out and discover their strengths, and the team may make up in productivity what it lacks in cohesiveness.

ASSERTION

This is an important and valuable development phase, but it can be tough for the leader. There will be challenges to the leadership. Team members have to find out that they can disagree with the leader before they will be willing to agree. They need to exercise their will internally, in order to hone it for team application externally. A good group leader will offer, and encourage team members to take, responsibilities and thereby satisfy their assertion needs. It is important that the leader allows the challenges, but unfortunately many leaders are threatened by them, and hunker down and assert their own authority in order to control the process. It requires a balancing act.

Those who run training groups often experience this phase of a five-day training group as the "kill the trainer" day. It generally begins toward the evening of the second day, but a good leader usually manages to be "resurrected" during the third day. If this phase coincides with the visit of an outside presenter, he may be given a very rough ride for little apparent reason! This is all a necessary, even healthy, part of group dynamics, but all too often, particularly among the reserved British, the interplays remain covert for the sake of appearances and they therefore take longer to work themselves out.

As I have said, a team in this phase can be quite productive, which may shield the recognition of yet greater potential. In fact, the majority of business or sports teams seldom advance beyond this phase, by and large because that is about as far as our whole western industrial society has collectively reached. To go beyond this is therefore to go above the norm, but that is not as difficult to achieve as is generally thought – with coaching.

## COOPERATION

At the beginning of this chapter we examined some of the most positive characteristics prevalent in the **cooperation** phase of a team. I do not wish to imply that such a team would be all sweetness and light. In fact, a danger of the cooperation stage is that an overemphasis on the group develops, which becomes too comfortable and does not allow for any dissent. The most productive teams will be highly cooperative but will retain a degree of dynamic tension. The best team leaders preserve this sensitively.

| Team development stage | | Characteristics | Maslow's hierarchy of needs |
|---|---|---|---|
| COOPERATION (performing) | Interdependent | Energy directed outward to common goals | Self-actualizing |
| (norming) | | | |
| ASSERTION (storming) | Independent | Energy focused on internal competition | Self-esteem / Esteem from others |
| INCLUSION (forming) | Dependent | Energy turned inward within team members | Belonging |

The figure opposite shows, in parentheses, another set of labels for the same team developmental sequence, and also some of the main distinguishing team characteristics. There are more.

For example, if a team is in the cooperation stage and one of its members has a bad day, the others will rally round and support. If it is in the assertion stage, the others may quietly celebrate the fall of a competitor. If it is in the inclusion stage, few will know or care.

On the other hand, if a team is in the cooperation stage and a team member has a personal triumph, the rest will join in the celebration. However, if the team is in the assertion stage, the rest may become jealous. If the team is in the inclusion stage, the others could even feel threatened.

We looked extensively at Maslow's model in Chapter 13, and the top three needs in individual development terms run parallel to the Firo B model. A team of self-actualizing individuals, if they could be found, would quickly attain the dizzy heights of cooperation and outstanding results. A team of those seeking self-esteem would perform very well individually but would be inclined to "do their own thing." People seeking the esteem of others would compete strongly against each other, producing some great performances – and some losers. A team of individuals seeking to belong would be compliant and irritatingly helpful, more in words than deeds.

Of course, the divisions between these three stages are permeable and overlapping, and the position and state of the team are subject to fluctuation when there is any turnover in team personnel.

MASLOW'S HIERARCHY OF NEEDS

Few readers will fail to recognize these stages and their characteristics from their own experience at work or at play. One macrocosmic example to challenge your mind is the suggestion that the whole of western industrial society is in the latter days of the assertion stage, with a few early signs of cooperation showing through (concern for the environment; the development of European integration). The collapse of the Soviet empire was the inevitable result of the attempt to coerce

THE MACROCOSM

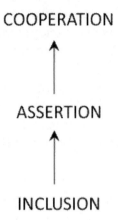

COOPERATION

ASSERTION

INCLUSION

How can the coach
facilitate/accelerate this process?

that society into the cooperation stage without allowing organic development through the previous stages. And the early attempts to redraw the map in eastern Europe and elsewhere were a manifestation of a temporary backslide into inclusion issues. For some, even survival and safety are in the foreground.

So if we can accept the idea that development of this general nature is common among teams of all shapes and sizes, it follows that we can resist and thereby retard team development, or we can encourage and accelerate it.

TEAMS TODAY

It could be said that at the start of the twenty-first century it is even more difficult to get the best out of a team. The reasons for this include the following:

- People no longer work in settled groupings but are continually forming and re-forming teams.
- Some teams are spread across geographic boundaries, making contact more infrequent and more problematic.
- The time scales within which teams are expected to join, form, and perform to meet a business challenge are shorter than ever before.

- The business challenges themselves have increased in complexity.
- Not all groups of people who collaborate need to be in a team to achieve their objectives.

The result is that coaching has a very important role to play in helping people to work well together. For example, it can help people establish whether and when they need to be in a team. Both groups and teams are valid ways of working and coaching applies to both. How it is best used with teams is addressed in the following chapter.

# 17
# Coaching Teams

*A manager only has two functions: first to get the job done and second to develop people*

It is said that a manager only has two functions: first to get the job done and second to develop his people. As I have said before, all too often managers are too busy doing the first to get around to the second. However, both functions are combined when coaching is used as the management style. So it is in teams – when the team is managed by coaching the job gets done well and the team develops at the same time. We will look here, however, at different applications of team coaching for task performance and for team development. The coaching of a team to perform a task is based on the same principles as coaching individuals. The more aware a team is both individually and collectively, the better it will perform.

TASK PERFORMANCE

Imagine that a business team is tackling a new task. The team leader may coach its members together by asking them questions. If it is a large group or team, the leader might ask rhetorical questions and get the team members in pairs or trios to discuss their responses with each other and then report on their conclusions to the whole group. He might mix people with different functions for this process to stimulate new ideas. He might himself participate in one of the pairs or trios.

By this method the team members would formulate their various **goals**. They would all provide the necessary input to a clear understanding of the **reality**. The resources and ideas of the whole team are employed to brainstorm the **options** and an agreed action plan is reached and driven forward by the combined **will** of the group. Of course, the team leader not only asks the coaching questions but gives his own input at any time. Such a process does take a little longer than a prescriptive team briefing, but the performance of the task will be incomparably better if all resources are pooled and the whole team becomes aware and responsible.

In some situations the team leader will group coach, for example in reviewing the team's past performance of a task. He may do this with all team members responding to his questions, but he might also ask them to write rather than speak their responses. This enables each of them at the same time to examine in detail their individual contribution to the overall task.

The questions might run as follows:

* What was the most difficult/time-consuming/stressful part of the task for you?
* How long did it take?
* What was difficult about it?
* What would you do differently next time?
* Who needs to know about the changes you will make?
* What support do you need? From whom? How will you get it?
* If you did that, how might it affect the result/the others/the quality/the time?

Each team member can then briefly share with the others what they came up with and resolve any conflicting changes. This process is very thorough, it brings out detail, it ensures clarity and understanding, it draws on all the team's resources, it promotes ownership and commitment, and it builds self-esteem and self-motivation.

To some team managers all this may sound unnecessary at best, and a load of rubbish at worst. Some will continue to believe that participation, involvement, self-esteem, shared responsibility, satisfaction, and quality of life in the workplace are "luxuries we can ill afford" and that they contribute nothing to performance. The arguments given here will not of themselves convince them otherwise, but in time their dwindling, disaffected workforce and their inability to build teams may.

## COACHING BY EXAMPLE

It is most important for a manager to establish the "right" kind of relationship with the team members under his charge from the moment he meets them. His behavior will be taken by the team members as the model for their behavior. They will tend to emulate him, even though initially they are likely to do so primarily as a means of gaining his approval while they are in the inclusion stage of team development.

If the team leader wishes to establish openness and honesty in the team, then he needs to be open and honest from the outset. If he wants the team members to trust him and each other, he must demonstrate trust and trustworthiness. If he sees the benefit in social contact among the team outside work, then he needs to participate in and perhaps initiate it himself.

Since the majority of individuals and teams still expect somewhat autocratic leadership, they might be surprised, even confused, by a leader who begins on a very participative note. A few might even imagine him to be weak or unsure of himself. It is advisable for him to pre-empt this on day one by describing his intended management style and inviting questions about it.

The manager or team leader also needs to be clear about his own willingness to invest time and energy in developing his team with a view to quality long-term relationships and performance, as opposed to merely getting the job done in the short term. If the manager only pays lip service to team-building principles, he will get no more than he pays for. Dedication to team process pays off.

## THE APPLICATION OF COACHING IN TEAMS

The Firo B team development model described in Chapter 16 forms an excellent basis for the application of coaching in teams. If the manager or coach understands that teams perform at their best when they reach the cooperation stage, he will use coaching with the team as a whole and with individual members to generate upward progress through the stages. For example, if the agreed **goal** is to lift the team into the cooperation stage and the **reality** is that it is now somewhere between the inclusion and assertion stages, what **options** do we have and what **will** we do?

The list of **options** that follows has been compiled from the responses to that question given by participants in the team-building programs that I run.

OPTIONS TO ACHIEVE TEAM COOPERATION

- **Discuss and agree the definition of a set of common goals for the team** This should be done within the team regardless of whether the organization has defined the team's goal. There is always room for modification and for deciding how it should be done. Each team member should be invited to contribute and also to add any personal goals that might be embraced within the overall team goal.
- **Develop a set of ground rules or operating principles acceptable to all team members and to which all have contributed** All should agree to abide by these even if they are not wholeheartedly behind every one of them. If they want to have their wishes included, it is essential that they agree to respect those of others. These ground rules should be subject to regular checking as to whether they are being adhered to and whether they need to be changed or updated. If all parties agree these rules in sincerity and have good intentions, harsh recriminations should not be made for lapses unless they become frequent.

Many of the suggestions that follow could be included as ground rules, but I will continue to list them separately.

- **Set aside time on a regular basis, usually in conjunction with a scheduled task meeting, for group process work** During this time ground rules are reviewed, appreciations and gripes are expressed, and personal sharing might be included so that openness and trust are built, and also so that team members are acknowledged as people, not just as cogs in a production machine. This period should not be allowed to be taken over by task talk.

- **Canvass team members' views about the desirability of arranging structured social time together** If a regular event is planned, the preference of an individual not to attend because of prior commitments or to respect the need for more family should be acknowledged. He, on the other hand, needs to be prepared for some feeling of separateness as a consequence of his choice.

- **Put support systems in place to deal, in confidence if requested, with individual troubles or concerns as they arise** If process meetings cannot be held frequently for geographic or other reasons, a buddy system might be instituted whereby each member of the team has another member as a buddy to whom they can talk if necessary. This way minor issues can be resolved promptly and valuable process meeting time is not wasted.

- **Develop a common interest outside work** Some teams have found that a group activity such as a sport or a common interest outside work that is shared by all can be very binding for the team. I recall one team who "adopted" a child in a developing country and, with a small monthly contribution each, paid for her schooling. They felt that she had contributed even more to their lives than they had to hers.

- **Learn a new skill together** Similar to the option above but more task oriented, some teams have agreed to learn a new skill such as coaching, or a language, or to attend a work-related course together. This might even be in healthy competition with other regional teams, for example, in the same organization.

- **Practice the qualities exercise together** Team relationships benefit greatly from team members doing appropriate variations among themselves of the qualities exercise explained in Chapter 17. This throws light on certain qualities, thereby helping to grow them. It also builds trust, understanding, and openness among team members remarkably quickly. It can be repeated in similar or different forms on a regular basis, for example at every other process meeting.

* **Hold group discussions on individual and collective meaning and purpose as perceived by group members** This is both broader and deeper than exploring goals. Meaning and purpose are what drive people, and a lack of them leads to lethargy, depression, and poor health. Throwing more light or awareness on something so pervasive that we are barely conscious of it will increase purposefulness and the quality of life at work and at home.

Each of these suggestions or **options** can be considered by the team using a coaching approach. That is to say that they may be introduced or quietly facilitated by the team leader, but should be decided on by the team members themselves. The decision to adopt one or more of them must be made democratically, but it also must be specific and recorded in ways recommended in Chapter 10. Remember that the basis of coaching to improve team performance is not imposing but increasing individual and collective **awareness** and **responsibility**.

# 18
# Overcoming Barriers to Coaching

*The greatest barrier is the inability to give up what you have done before*

We have looked at the context of coaching, its value, and its irrefutable logic. There is no mystique about coaching. It is not difficult to learn. However, it cannot be learned from a book, any more than driving a car or a golf ball can. Like all skills, it requires practice. If that practice is undertaken with commitment, and with **awareness** and **responsibility**, you do not need long to become proficient and relaxed in its use, and to benefit from its results.

A NEW VISION OF PEOPLE

For some people, coaching both demands and causes a fundamental change in the way they perceive themselves and others, be they colleagues, subordinates, or competitors. To see all people as having the potential to be great in their chosen field, just as an acorn has in its field, is a far cry from the more common but outmoded perception of people as empty vessels of little worth until given outside input. That shift may take time for some prospective coaches or it may come as a revelation, but even before it takes place, and while the underlying philosophy still seems foreign, it is possible to raise performance levels quite effectively by simply following the principles of good coaching prescribed in this book.

Nothing is plain sailing, however, and you are liable to meet a few barriers along the way. The greatest barrier without a doubt is not the inability to coach but the inability to give up telling, to give up what you have done before in each circumstance, to give up your old habitual management or teaching behavior. One you have conquered that one you can begin.

The most frequently expressed concern is: "How do I coach resistant people?" This is very often raised, but more in fear and anticipation than from any actual negative experiences. If coaching is introduced sensitively, it is often accepted with no difficulty or, better still, welcomed. That is not to say that everyone readily accepts coaching, nevertheless. Any change of behavior by a coach or manager is viewed with fear and suspicion by some and may be met with a level of resistance. Most people have a long history of being told by parents, by school teachers, and by their first bosses, so naturally they expect to be told and may find it strange being asked for their opinion. Another way of looking at the resistance is to consider what they are really resisting; it is, of course, becoming more aware or more responsible and the consequences of both. You can then coach people on recognizing the source of their resistance and on overcoming it.

I suggested above that it is easier to learn the new – the basics of coaching – than it is to give up the old – telling. We are conditioned by a long history of telling and being told; so are the people we coach. The expectation and therefore the wish to be told are ingrained in all of us, even if there are benefits to being asked. It is no bad thing to explain to and remind those we manage or coach what the benefits to them personally are: learning to think for themselves, greater awareness in all things that enhances performance, learning and enjoyment, more choice, a greater sense of responsibility, enhanced self-belief, possible promotion, and learning to self-coach and to coach others in and out of the workplace. While the benefits are legion, there may still be resistance.

When our parents asked us questions, it was often because we had done something wrong. There was no safe answer to "Why did you do that?" – we were in trouble anyway. When our schoolteachers asked us questions, it was to test either our knowledge or whether we had been paying attention. In either case it was important to get the answer right, so questions themselves came to be seen as a threat.

It is not surprising, therefore, that to some people coaching questions are intimidating too, and so the coach must put them at their ease, build trust, and be nonjudgmental about their responses. It may also help simply to explain and demonstrate that the purpose of coaching questions is to raise awareness, not to test. There are seldom "right" answers to coaching questions, just honest ones.

If resistance persists, coachees are either resisting being more aware or being more responsible, probably because they feel that these will take them out of their comfort zone. They may be afraid that questions will cause them to reveal to themselves or others the ghosts that they fear lurk within their psyche. Childhood conditioning may have taught them never to show their emotions or any other human weakness lest someone should take advantage of them. However irritating their paranoia may be, a patient and compassionate approach is likely to be the best way forward.

Of course, there are some people who are difficult about most things. This may stem from deep hostility toward the company or the manager, or toward people in general for some reason. The more likely scenario is simply a reluctant employee who wants to do enough to get by and no more: "That is all I'm paid for. Don't ask me to think things out for myself. You're the manager, you're paid to do that."

This is hard to change, but the key is the fact that people with such an attitude can't enjoy their working lives. A softly, softly approach that helps them to discover that their quality of life in the workplace may improve if they cooperate with coaching is probably the only way. Bring coaching questions in so gradually that the person doesn't even know he is being coached; in fact he is not at this stage, you are merely asking him questions a little more frequently than you did before.

The barriers below are drawn from lists created by participants during our coaching programs. They are all expressed here as if they are real rather than assumed and constructed by the manager or potential coach. Of course, if they are perceived as real they are effectively real until they can be recognized as a personal concern within which lies some truth.

I have listed the barriers in external and internal categories, in the way course participants tend to divide them. I will make a few comments on each and repeat some mentioned above to show how they are usually categorized.

## EXTERNAL BARRIERS

**The company culture is against this kind of approach**
Of course it is, to some extent, or you would not only now be introducing coaching. A coaching philosophy is part of the new company culture that the enlightened people in your organization are trying to create. Others prefer the boring illusion of the security of the status quo. However, more and more organizations are coming to the conclusion that survival in future may depend on change now, and that the status quo is actually the riskier alternative.

**People are cynical of any new approach**
Yes, some of them probably will be, especially if communication within your organization has not been the best. It is important to tell them what you will do differently, and why.

**They won't understand what I'm doing and won't trust me**
Same as the one above.

**They'll know I've been on a course and give me a few weeks to get back to "normal"**
Same as the one above.

**They'll think it's just a new management gimmick**
Explain that it is not a gimmick, but a necessity for improved performance and better staff relations. They will soon discover that it is no gimmick, unless that is how you yourself see it.

**It takes too long – I would rarely have the time to coach**

It all depends when you start and when you stop the timer. In the moment it is usually quicker to tell people what to do, but if they immediately forget and you have to tell them again… and again… and again, or if you have to keep looking over their shoulder, which takes longer?

Let me quote a user of coaching, a production-plant manager with a pharmaceutical company.

*Everything I do is essentially performance-aimed. I use coaching as a means of getting my staff to a level where I can delegate work to them which I would otherwise have to do myself. I see the time I spend coaching very much as an investment, the dividend from which is the far greater time I save myself through delegation.*

*If there is a fire, I won't hesitate to yell "Get out of here!" but unless I actively seek opportunities to GROW my staff by coaching them, I will be stuck in the fire-fighting cycle.*

**They expect to be told**

If they have always been told in the past, then they will expect to be told. That is not the same thing as preferring to be told.

**They want to be told – they don't want responsibility**

If people have never been given responsibility by their parents, at school, or at work, it will seem scary at first, like anything new. Underneath, the majority of us crave responsibility, in part because it provides us with a measure of self-worth. Those with very low self-worth have a hard time with responsibility. It is another cycle to get stuck in, but coaching is the best way I know to help people out of it. A few of the relevant coaching questions might be:

- What do you want from work apart from money?
- What does responsibility mean to you?
- Do you feel a burden of responsibility right now?
- Is responsibility always a burden to you?
- What do you think some people like about responsibility?
- What else are you responsible for in your life?
- What are you afraid of?

- What could you do to overcome that?
- What are you willing to take responsibility for?
- Are you willing to try accepting more responsibility for a week?

Merely by answering these questions, they are beginning to take on responsibility – at least for their own answers and choices. If you, as their manager, won't help them to take responsibility, who will? And are you satisfied with the minimal performance that an irresponsible person provides?

**They'll think I've gone nuts**
They may! So what? Madness is so endearing! Just explain.

**I'll lose my authority**
A manager who manages by coaching gains real respect, as well as self-respect, which is far more gratifying than the illusion of power that props up autocrats until they fade or fall.

**I'm an expert and they respect and expect my knowledgeable input**
Your expertise will still be invaluable; only the way you use it will change. Do you begrudge others acquiring some of it from you? Do you dispense your knowledge in small bites, so no one can get enough of it to threaten you? Or do you want to encourage your would-be successors to stand on your shoulders?

**I already use a coaching style – I don't need to change anything**
One of the classic ways of avoiding having to change is to claim that you already do it. Such people usually have a very poor version of coaching buried somewhere in the bottom of their managerial kitbag. To find out if they use it, ask their subordinates. But be careful, this may also be one of your own internal barriers. Is it? See below.

## INTERNAL BARRIERS

**It's nothing new – I've done it for years**
If this is your arrogant response, then for certain you haven't!

**I'm afraid I won't do it well**
Without practice you won't. Self-coaching is the least risky place to start. Try it out with the five-a-side football team or with your son or daughter. At work there will be some individuals and teams who are easier to work with than others. Try it out with them, and tell them what you are doing.

**I'll get stuck – I won't know what question to ask**
This won't happen if you follow the golden rule of listening to and watching the coachee, and following their interest, lead, or direction. They will always indicate what you should ask. Remember you are an awareness raiser, not an instructor. Keep it simple; the whole process is simply variations on the following theme:

| | |
|---|---|
| What do you want? | **Goal** |
| What is happening? | **Reality** |
| What could you do? | **Options** |
| What will you do? | **Will** |

**I won't get the results I get with my old style**
No, you won't. You will soon get better ones!

Most perceived external obstacles have a major internal component

**What I did before worked, why change?**
Because the survival of your organization and yourself may be dependent on better performance and better quality of life in the workplace.

**I don't believe in these new softly, softly approaches**
Too bad, but have you ever tried using one?

**The only thing that motivates people is money**
Ample recent research shows that this is not true, but it may appear to be until you learn how to offer them something more meaningful.

Now add your own list of internal barriers to this section, but simply precede each one with the phrase "The belief I hold that…" I do not suggest that your external barriers have no validity out there, but you would do well to acknowledge that a goodly portion of them are internal ones.

We all prefer to believe that *they* are the problem; it makes us right and saves us having to change. But it also means we are stuck with the situation because we can't change *them*. If we can admit that it may be our own resistance that we project on to them, we are empowered to change things, because *they* are now under our control!

This is just another instance of self-**awareness** and of taking **responsibility** leading to improved managerial performance.

No matter how much better the new might be, letting go of the old symbols of our security is always hard. But learning and adopting new behaviors demand that we let go of old ones. The system and skill of coaching are simple and not hard to learn. Letting go of a well-used command-and control habit to make room for coaching is much harder. I find it is often more productive to allocate time and focus to provoking and assisting people to let go of the old rather than to teaching the new. Once they do let go of the old, the new rushes in to fill the vacuum. Remove the blocks and the potential emerges.

So often it is when we let go of the need for control that we gain control

Coaching is, after all, a natural skill and one that perhaps does not have to be taught at all if the opening is there. Loving parents who have never learned to coach use it very effectively with their children for everything from tying shoelaces to doing maths homework. They use it with their children because they care for them and about their learning and growth. If managers cared a little more for their staff, they would use coaching naturally too. If executives cared a little more for their managers than for their bottom line, even they might coach – and the bottom line would take care of itself.

# 19
# The Multiple Benefits of Coaching

*You can make a man run, but you can't make him run fast*

So what, then, are the benefits of coaching as opposed to instructing to the manager and the managed, and what are the benefits to an organization of adopting what I call a coaching culture?

**Improved performance and productivity**
This must be number one, and we would not do it if it did not work. Coaching brings out the best in individuals and in teams, something that instructing does not even aspire to do, so how could it?

**Staff development**
As I have stated earlier, developing people does not mean just sending them on a short course once or twice a year. The way you manage will either develop them or hold them back. It's up to you.

**Improved learning**
Coaching is learning on the fast track, without loss of time from the bench or desk. Enjoyment and retention are also enhanced.

## Improved relationships

The very act of asking someone a question values them and their answer. If I only tell, there is no exchange. I might as well be talking to a load of bricks. I once asked a particularly silent but promising junior tennis player what he thought was good about his forehand. He smiled and said, "I don't know. Nobody has ever asked me my opinion before." That said it all to me.

## Improved quality of life for individuals

Because of the respect for individuals, the improved relationships, and the success that will accompany coaching, the atmosphere at work will change for the better.

## More time for the manager

Staff who are coached, who welcome responsibility, do not have to be chased or watched, freeing managers to perform their more overarching functions, which in the past they never found the time to do well.

## More creative ideas

Coaching and a coaching environment encourage creative suggestions from all members of a team without the fear of ridicule or premature dismissal. One creative idea often sparks off others.

## Better use of people, skills, and resources

A manager very often has no idea what hidden resources are available to him until he starts coaching. He will soon uncover many previously undeclared talents in his team as well as solutions to practical problems, which can only be found by those who have to carry out a task regularly.

## Faster and more effective emergency response

In an atmosphere in which people are valued, they are invariably willing to push the boat out when or even before being called on to do so. In far too many organizations, where people are not valued they only do what they are told, and as little as possible at that.

### Greater flexibility and adaptability to change

The coaching ethos is all about change, being responsive and responsible. In future the demand for flexibility will increase, not decrease. Increased competition in the market, technological innovation, instant global communication, economic uncertainty and social instability will see to that throughout our brief lifetime! Only the flexible and resilient will survive.

### More motivated staff

I repeat here that both the carrot and the stick have lost their edge and that people perform because they want to, not because they have to. Coaching helps people to discover their self-motivation.

### Culture change

The coaching principles underpin the management style of the high-performance culture to which so many business leaders aspire. Any coaching program will help make culture transformation more realizable.

### A life skill

Coaching is both an attitude and a behavior, with multiple applications both in and out of work. It is more and more in demand, so even those who are looking to change their job soon are going to find it an invaluable skill wherever they go.

## COACHING TO WIN

Sports coaching is at last deserting its behavioral roots. Coaches are increasingly replacing, or at least enhancing, their old instructional style by focusing more on the person than the technique, on the potential rather than on the mistake. This approach creates a far better mental state that is the precondition for natural learning to take place, for bio-mechanical efficiency to emerge rather than a prescribed one-size-fits-all technique. A recent and highly significant example of this trend was profiled in the extraordinary success of the British cyclists in the 2008 Olympics in Beijing. Their performance director, Dave Brailsford, explained, "I've always been a firm believer in the carrot and not the stick. I don't believe in humiliating, dictating or controlling; it's more about mentoring and supporting."

Later in 2008 a Welsh Rugby coach and later an English soccer coach told me two very similar stories reflecting an observation that Tim Gallwey had made that led him to the Inner Game all those years ago. Tim had said of his tennis pupils, "I noticed that the less I taught, the more they learned." The two team coaches both reported occasions when for different reasons, their teams were largely left to their own devices the week before a big match, instead of doing their usual intensive training. On each of these occasions they played their best game and achieved the best results of the season. Why? Because the players were responsible for their own preparation and performance – the player-centered approach. I will let them tell the stories.

Head coach Richard Hodges describes here an experience with his Glamorgan Wanderers Rugby team:

*The traditionally mid-table Glamorgan Wanderers were approaching their last two matches in the 2008 Welsh Premiership. The first one was an away midweek game and the players all had proper jobs anyway, so their manager and coach "mothered them, made all their decisions for them and hardly let them breathe for themselves." They lost the match badly.*

*For the final match of the season a week later the management decided to take the opposite tactic, the player centred approach. They told them, "Unless there are problems, you won't see us at all. In preparation for the match, you choose whatever you want to do. If you want to spend your time in the pub, that's up to you." It was outside the comfort zone for some inevitably. They decided that they still wanted to do their regular training sessions, but they ran it themselves. When the match came, at half time they were losing 12–15 and the captain, not the coach, led the short debrief. They went on to play their best match ever and win 34–15 against all expectations. They unanimously attributed their success to be entirely due to the fact that they had taken total ownership of their game.*

This is what Tony Falkner, Performance Coach at Blackburn Rovers FC Academy, had to say in the other example.

*In preparing for a game we pay attention to the emotional state of the team, we are acutely aware of how this can affect the team positively or negatively. For one particular game we had not trained Monday through to Thursday with only a mental preparation session in the classroom on Friday afternoon. The coaching staff were apprehensive about going into the game with so little technical, tactical and physical preparation. We won 3–0 and put in a great performance.*

*Three weeks later we found ourselves in the same position, no training all week, short yet concise mental preparation session on the Friday afternoon. Same thoughts and feelings from the coaching staff. We won 4–0 again with a very good performance. This started us thinking: the players had not been exposed to any interference leading up to the game from the expectations of the coach. The balance between the interference that a prescriptive style of coaching can create and how through "coaching" we affect the performance positively must be understood.*

A few courageous mavericks began experimenting with this approach with team sports 20 years earlier. One was David Whitaker, who later joined David Hemery and me in Performance Consultants. He used "new" coaching with the British field hockey team in the 1988 Olympics in Seoul. When he first took on the task as team coach he had been an international player himself for years, and the team would always wait for his directions before they started their training. Later, they started without him. They learned to coach each other; for example, the defenders began coaching the attackers and vice versa. He systematically coached the team to take responsibility for much of their own training methods and schedules. He said of the team: "They became a harmonious, dynamic unit without negating the special individual talents that each player contributed."

They were doing so well with this process that he light-heartedly suggested that they did not need him to come to Seoul at all and he gave them the choice. They did, however, want him to come, they said, "to carry their bags." They won the gold.

So how do these principles and examples from sport translate into the world of work? This story is from an article by Cari Tuna that appeared in the *Wall Street Journal* in November 2008.

*Two years ago, Greg Cushard was leading eight or nine meetings a week at Rubicon Oil Co., the truck-refueling company he founded and runs. He would interrupt conversations among subordinates, identify mistakes and make even mundane decisions, he says.*

*"I acted like a quarterback... more than a coach," Cushard says. He had little time to think about the business. Employees "stopped making suggestions because they were afraid they'd get shot down."*

*Prompted by advice from his top lieutenants and executive coach, Cushard resolved to stop micromanaging. He started leaving meetings after briefly setting the tone and agenda. He soon stopped attending some altogether, appointing others to lead in his place. Rubicon... has about 40 employees. "They did not want me there," Cushard says. "My presence hindered thinking."*

*Today, Rubicon employees take turns running meetings. Leaders periodically follow up with co-workers, creating more accountability within departments, Mr. Cushard says.*

*He now attends three or four meetings a week; subordinates send updates from the rest. In his newfound spare time, Cushard launched a second company, a fuel clearinghouse that tracks oil prices.*

*As owners, "we think we know best, but we don't, not all of the time," he says. "I realized that it's not all about me."*

## THE FIELD GUN RACE

Here is another awesome example of the immense value of these principles, from an activity that could hardly be called sport but it is not the workplace either in the normal sense of the word.

The Field Gun race was the highlight of the Royal Tournament, a great military show that used to be held each summer in London. The contestants were teams from different branches of the British Navy. Initiated many years ago to commemorate a heroic campaign in the Boer War in which artillery was manhandled over mountains, the event consisted of a race to partially dismantle and drag an ancient gun and gun carriage over an obstacle course that would be daunting enough to most of us without any baggage. This competition was renowned for the great strength required, the number of injuries in training and its tradition of autocratic leadership, which produced remarkable performances but was diametrically opposed to the coaching philosophy. The teams were only allowed nine weeks to assemble and train their 16-man teams.

In 1990, Joe Gough was the first trainer for the Fleet Air Arm team. Before training started, he attended a two-day Performance Coaching course run by David Hemery and me, after which, with considerable courage, Joe decided to change his approach radically. Subsequently David visited the team in Southampton early in their training and was impressed with how effective Joe was, or rather the team was. What happened? For the first time in the history of the event this one service won all five major trophies.

The Fleet Air Arm A team recorded the fastest time, the best aggregate time, the most points, and the fewest penalties, and the B team also won its trophy. This outstanding result was achieved with 30 percent fewer practice runs than in previous years and with fewer injuries. After the event Joe said, "We changed everything this year, and if we'd failed I'd have been pilloried, but right now I'm the most popular man in the Fleet Air Arm!" When asked to explain their success, he said, "The way we did it before, we had one brain, and sixteen bodies, now we used seventeen brains." They went on to win all five trophies for the next two years as well.

Here are some quotes from the team at the time:

* "This was the first time that someone had asked our opinion and listened."
* "Joe would ask us if we wanted to do another run, and if we said no, we felt we owed him a bit, and that was a positive carry-over to the next day."
* "Joe was very approachable. He treated us like men."
* "One night Joe told us to rig up for another run, and we were shattered. Eric, our PTI, went and told Joe that he and

the team thought his decision was wrong. Joe came out and told us to stow the gear away! I couldn't believe it. It takes a big man to admit he was wrong… and once he had done that, the rest of us started admitting that we had been wrong on parts of our drill practices, instead of making excuses. There was a lot more honesty all round."

Joe Gough summed up his new-found conviction that coaching really does produce better performances than commanding and fear can when he said: "You can make a man run, but you can't make him run fast!"

The Field Gun race has been described as the toughest team competition in the world and I have seen nothing to challenge it. The successes described here are indeed an extraordinary endorsement of the use of the coaching principles with teams, because they show the mental and emotional factors to be of primary importance; coaching values people and their ability to self-manage.

# Part III

# Leadership for High Performance

# 20
# The Challenge to Leaders

*Could the only thing limiting us be the size of our vision and our own self-limiting beliefs?*

This fourth edition of *Coaching for Performance* comes at a time when humanity is facing huge challenges in the economy, in the environment, in the widening gap between rich and poor, and in social stress and distress. Though this is a book about coaching, it would be a grave omission not to acknowledge the broader business and social conditions that exist, and for which coaching has so much to offer. Where there is confusion, coaching can bring clarity. Where there is fear, coaching can build trust. Where there is concern, coaching can bring hope. Where there is isolation, coaching can bring connection. Where there is competition, coaching can bring cooperation.

We are beset by many unknowns. How will we manage in the future? Will we revert to command and control as fear increases and as the economic pendulum swings? I believe that humanity is still destined to travel a positive evolutionary journey, but that we have veered way off track, seduced by materialism and consumerism, and that course corrections are urgently needed. If good sense, and a little coaching, will not get us back on track, then ever more alarming credit and climate crunches may force us to, but not without much pain and suffering. How will business react? What are the role and responsibility of business? What indeed will the purpose of business be in the future? Will the mega multinational corporations rule the world or will a new cadre of political leaders with real vision and values retake the high ground? Where are the Abraham Lincolns, Winston Churchills, Mahatma Gandhis, or Nelson Mandelas of the future?

While we wait in vain for a savior, might it not be wise for us to take more responsibility for ourselves, for others, and for our future? Who will be the next generation of leaders? What attributes will they have? I suggest that the evolutionary journey of our species has reached the stage at which the hierarchies of the past are due to be replaced by a new form of devolved leadership and collective res-ponsibility. Could it be that the coaching profession has emerged and grown so fast in only 25 years because it meets this broader need for self-responsibility, which, after all, is its principal product? Could the coaching profession have emerged to help to midwife a new era, or is that too grand a notion? Could the only thing limiting us be the size of our vision and our own self-limiting beliefs?

If you think I am being too utopian, let us consider what others have had to say. George Orwell, Stanley Kubrick, and even Alvin Toffler would tell us that prediction is a risky business, but that when the signs are strong enough it does no harm to be aware of the possibilities. Since to change the management culture of large organizations takes many years, it is vital for leaders to look into the future. One way to do this is to examine what an individual's process of psychological development can tell us about the direction in which companies, communities, and cultures are evolving, and the stages through which they will pass on the journey. Indeed, the central platform of Arie de Geus's groundbreaking book *The Living Company* is that companies are and act like living beings.

Can businesses experience the same kind of crisis of meaning that many individuals are currently undergoing? I suggest that they can and they do. And could it be more widespread still? Could the corporate world, or the world itself, be approaching a collective crisis of meaning? There are many telltale signs. Economic indicators are no longer providing clear signals of what is happening. The environment, the unstable economy, and declining corporate ethics are posing immediate, unprecedented challenges to business, but business is not responding, paralyzed by its old paradigms and by the need for immediate crisis management. In the view of many, a greater crisis is here now, and denial of it is rife.

Let us face it, despite the wise words, warnings, and exhortations of a few exceptional economists, many scientists, and even some politicians and corporate leaders, the problems facing humanity have continued to worsen. My deep disappointment is how painfully slowly and inadequately all of us have responded to the blindingly obvious. When will we turn words into actions? Or will an inconceivably severe manmade or natural crisis have to occur to awaken us?

## COACHING THE CORPORATION

The rest of this chapter is retained almost unchanged from when I wrote it for the third edition, specifically to show how little has changed in the intervening time and how valid the content remains. It will take you from the big picture of business to the local and practical applications of coaching, while always maintaining the theme of the need and the reasons for change.

The UK has led the way in attempting to address the problem of poverty by writing off some third world debt, an idea that was unthinkable when Fidel Castro suggested it in the 1980s. Bill Gates, the ultimate marketeer, has now recognized that computers do not keep people alive and is setting an example by generously funding a global immunization program. A special edition of *Newsweek* devoted to issues that would dominate the world identified globalization as the main influence. There were two related concerns: that private business will have to carry more of the public burden in trying

GLOBALIZATION

to repair social problems, and that the market is not the answer to everything.

Claude Smadja of the World Economic Forum wrote:

*Private companies must assert a much wider and stronger sense of corporate social responsibility. And we must listen to the responsible voices of a new "civil society"… The rise of NGOs also reflects increased public disenchantment with all institutions – governments, corporations, international organizations, media.*

Michael Hirsh of *Newsweek* commented that the debate is less about privatizing the public sector than the converse, "publicizing" the private sector.

Manny Armadi, CEO of Cause & Effect Marketing in the UK, expressed it another way:

*The burden of economic fundamentals is now such that government on its own can't fulfil its social obligations. On the other side, the sheer power and influence of businesses in the economy is now huge.*

When asked if he thought people were entitled to hold the leaders of such enterprises accountable for their behavior, he replied, "Absolutely."

Globalization and instant, frequent communication around the world are blurring the space and time distinctions between "us" and "them." At the same time, our continually, though some would argue slowly, maturing consciousness is causing us to extend our area of concern to include within "us" people, countries, and cultures that a decade ago we would certainly have regarded as "them." Thus both external forces and our inner development are conspiring to break down barriers and persuade us to accept and embrace the common destiny that all people share – and share responsibility for.

## CORPORATE SOCIAL RESPONSIBILITY

So if the public is calling for more corporate social responsibility and inspiring business leaders are talking about it, why is so little of it happening? What is the sticking point? Deborah Holmes of Ernst & Young confirmed something I have observed on many of my coaching courses when she said:

*You can have very enlightened practices in the heads of the top leaders, and employees hungry for enlightened practices. And then managers are operating the way they always have, not understanding that there's anything more to their responsibility than a good profit-and-loss statement.*

Clearly, these issues were around well before the devastating attack on the World Trade Center in New York on 11 September 2001. However, for many individuals, businesses, and nations, that event triggered new and even deeper consideration of personal and collective responsibility and may have accelerated the changes already envisaged by earlier commentators. The summarizing heading of a *Financial Times* article written before the attack is: "A reconnection with core values: Greed is not good in the new age of business: Workers are more than the sum of their parts: Spirituality in business: Stephen Overell joins the search for the ultimate competitive advantage, and finds that companies are trying to offer staff meaning and purpose."

Greed is not good in the new age of business

Jim McNish, head of executive development at retail group Kingfisher, is quoted in the article as saying, "Human beings want to love their organisations – they don't want to work for a set of bastards. People seek meaning in their work and will start to creep out the door if they find none." Ken Costa, vice-chairman of banking group UBS Warburg, makes a similar point: "You can see the frustration. It demonstrates itself in uncertainty and a lack of fulfilment and ultimately leads people to leave an organisation. More are leaving to work in the voluntary sector... In the last round of graduate recruitment we did, a surprising amount of people asked 'what are your policies regarding social responsibility'. That has never happened before."

Many people believe that a major shift in the attitude and role of business is inevitable and in fact is already under way, driven in large measure by public demand. People are signifying that they will no longer tolerate being in service to the economy; instead, they are demanding that the economy be made to serve people. Will this come about by a series of managed course corrections as businesses learn to accept their responsibility, their true meaning and purpose, or will they continue their blinkered pursuit of wealth at any price until they run into barricades manned by ordinary people with higher demands and aspirations?

Changes in ethics and values in society and in business affect a wide range of aspects of business relating to both people and products:

- The way staff are treated and management style.
- Treatment of the environment, such as waste and recycling.
- The way suppliers are treated, particularly those in developing countries.
- Fair remuneration for all, with an eye to executive excesses.
- Concerns about aggressive selling and misleading advertising.
- Internal and external openness and honesty.
- Health and welfare considerations for staff, including stress, the demands of parenting, and so on.
- Sexual equality, positive racial attitudes, and avoidance of harassment.
- Executives expected to be role models and set examples.
- Products that offer genuine value.
- Products that are socially beneficial, or at least neutral.
- Products that put people before profit.
- Concerns over the use of hazardous or environmentally dangerous chemicals.
- How the company relates to the wider community.

A company that disregards any of these areas is at risk of criticism and needs to bear in mind that even what is acceptable today may not be so tomorrow. A company with vision, however, will not just be keeping pace with the public mood but will want to be ahead of it, particularly because it realizes that it has a responsibility to society.

## COACHING FOR CULTURE CHANGE

A listening, learning, coaching culture may provide the best chance of riding out the unsettling waves of change that businesses are facing. Businesses can adopt a more supportive, people-oriented culture, one in which coaching is commonplace, downwards, with peers, and even upwards. In this way staff's needs are acknowledged and they are helped by coaching to clarify their direction for themselves, while at the same time the coach/manager learns a great deal about their wishes and hopes. If managers listen to their people and act on what they hear, employees will be happier and perform better and staff turnover will plummet. On the other hand, if they only pay lip service to this, they will have raised expectations only to dash them again and will have made things worse than they were before.

In addition to this management style change, companies are likely to be called on to live up to the values and ethics they so boldly claim in their mission statements. If they don't, they may be taken to task by their staff and their customers. Both are liable to vote with their feet. Companies providing products and services that make a genuine contribution to society offer meaningful employment by their very nature. Those whose products and services are questionable or downright harmful are most likely to fall foul of staff seeking meaning and purpose at work.

On this scale, few companies are wholly black and few wholly white. The majority are a shade of gray. The wiser ones can and do compensate for any perceived failings in various ways, for example by contributing to the local community or lending staff to social projects.

Why is coaching so important in this? Because a value-based future cannot be prescribed by some outside authority. Performance will always be at its best when staff, shareholders, directors, and even customers share the same values, but before that can happen staff need to be encouraged to find out what their own values are.

Once we accept that we need to change the culture of our business to incorporate a coaching ethos, where do we start?

A value-based future cannot be prescribed by some outside authority

With the people or with the company? The answer must be both. Imposing democracy and demanding cooperation are unacceptable contradictions. Here are a few guidelines:

- If we redesign our company structure too radically or too quickly, we are liable to get too far ahead of our staff.
- If we impose a redesign on our staff, they are liable to object even if it is intended to be entirely for their benefit.
- We must first help staff develop themselves and through coaching experiment with some of the attitudes and behaviours that we expect in the new organization.
- Executives and senior management must, from the very beginning, set an example and model the ideal attitudes and behaviors authentically and well.
- Staff cannot be forced to change, but need the opportunity to choose how to change.
- Without a collective vision change cannot succeed, but without vision at the top it will not even start.

## THE COACHING APPROACH

When coaching the board members of a company going through culture change, we must first help them to become clear about what they require from the change and what it involves, and ensure that they are fully committed to seeing it through. This is likely to require an investment of time that board members are often reluctant to make because of short-term pressures. However, lasting and effective change is only a pipe dream without the commitment of the board, or at the very least of one key member of it who acts as a champion. The willingness to see change through is vital to avoid staff becoming disillusioned if grand plans come to nothing.

The approach we take at Performance Consultants is then to institute a very thorough program of maintenance and reinforcement from day one to support managers' initial exposure to coaching and the accompanying management style changes expected of them. Every member of staff in any supervisory role must go through a basic coaching skills course to ensure that a new common language is quickly established. The rest of the staff will also need at least an explanation and some exposure to the principles of coaching so that they are not confused or suspicious of any behavioral changes on the part of managers.

Other components of culture change maintenance include regular updates, supervision, buddy sharing, feedback, assessment, appraisals, and support of many kinds. The more these are internally designed and staffed the better. We prefer to train "master coaches" within the organization to do this rather than undertaking it ourselves because then ownership lies where it needs to be – within the company.

Let us now turn our attention to the foundation of leadership, since both coaching and leadership have crucial roles to play in ringing the changes we so urgently need.

# 21
# The Foundation of Leadership

*The journey toward enlightened leadership is far from straightforward,*
*it is challenging, and it takes time*

Coaching leads us inexorably to leadership for four principal reasons:

- **Successful leaders of the future will have to lead in a coaching style rather than command and control** Staff retention, especially that of the best staff, is a vital issue and expectations about the way people are treated are rising fast. Prescription, instruction, autocracy, and hierarchy are losing traction and acceptability. Good people want more choice, more responsibility, and more fun in their lives, and that includes the workplace.

- **Management and leadership style determines the performance of staff and a coaching approach delivers the highest performance** What business would not like better performance? This is widely accepted intellectually in organizations, both in the public and the private sector, but they still struggle to embed and embody the behaviors they advocate. In many cases both leaders and followers collude to resist change even though that benefits neither.

- **As we help others to build their awareness, their responsibility, and consequently their self-belief, they**

**lay the foundation stones of their own future leadership capability** Leaders by definition have to make choices and decisions daily and to do so effectively, they require these fundamental personal attributes. Coaching builds leaders, and there is a dearth of leadership today, in every sector, in every institution, and in every country.

- **The external context within which organizations operate is changing fast, due in large measure to circumstances outside the control of the company or even the country** Globalization, instant communication, economic crises, corporate social responsibility, and huge environmental issues are a few obvious examples, and there are many more. Coping with these, along with the speed of change itself, demands new leadership qualities.

The shortage of good leaders applies in all fields, in corporations, in government, in education, in healthcare, in religion, indeed everywhere. There are also some truly exceptional leaders who have managed to extract themselves from the pile and shine in each of these sectors, although they are rare. Generally they were fortunate enough to have exceptional parenting or schooling or both, they took advantage of the opportunities they had, and they were probably more self-aware. We could say that they learned experientially from time and application in the University of Life. The rest were not so lucky, or not so wise. However, there is another very powerful factor: fear.

Would-be leaders face a multitude of external challenges that are often overwhelming and they can't see the wood for the trees. They had an unprecedentedly tough job even before the economic downturn, and they are ill equipped to cope. The skills that they were taught at business school or acquired as they climbed the corporate ladder have lost their relevance in the prevailing conditions, so it is not surprising that they have become fearful. They also live and work in a culture of fear, which further hampers them. Freedom from fear is their greatest need.

In recent years I have asked a large number of corporate leaders and senior managers who or what pushes them every

FREEDOM FROM FEAR

day to keep going, to put in extra effort, or to stay late at the office. They give three consistent answers: time, fear, and the bottom line, referring to next month's figures specifically. All of these are in fact fear related. It is no exaggeration to say that business itself exists in a paradigm of fear, and that fear needs to be addressed first.

Why should we expect leaders to be the best of the bunch in any case? They are often powerful, clever, cunning, rich, even daunting, but the best? What do we mean by best anyway? And best for what? The task of leadership and the skills leaders need will vary according to the circumstance of the time, but the essential nature of certain qualities remains constant, although these are the ones in short supply. Our formal education equips us with intellectual, technical, and academic knowledge, but it does not address personal or inner development. The result is that while many aspiring leaders have MBAs and a track record or two, few have actively engaged in personal development. While they may be clever, even brilliant, they frequently remain relatively immature psychologically, and it is mature leadership that we so urgently need.

Tap the ancient wisdom

Real leadership development in my book, and in this book, is neither intellectual nor academic, neither is it knowledge based nor technological, all of which are sourced from outside the person. The origins of the best coaching, the Inner Game, are all about eliminating our internal obstacles and drawing out the untapped bank of riches latent within each human being. It is not about putting more of someone else's knowledge in from outside. Few in western culture know of the wealth that is hidden within us, despite the traditions of ancient wisdom. The door to our wisdom vault is rusty with disuse and old furniture is piled up against it. We have to clear away the debris before we can open the door. That debris is years of parental, social, and cultural conditioning and all the false beliefs and assumptions that arise from it. One effect of all that is that we fear failure; we fear not meeting the expectations of our parents, of society, and now of ourselves.

If fear defines the inner state of most leaders, it is hardly surprising that they are failing. Fear can be attributed to external or to internal factors or both; however, whatever the external circumstances are, we are responsible for our reactions to them. We can succumb to them and wimp out, we can deny them and continue as if they don't exist, or we can take them as a challenge and rise to the occasion. The difference, or indeed the decision, is a matter of the stage of personal development the leader has reached. Only when the members of the board are free of their own fear reactions will they be able to build trust with the next layer of managers, and so on down through a company.

They will often first attempt to change the external circumstances that generate their fear, and sometimes they will succeed, but the relief is short lived. A new circumstance arises or old ones reappear before they know it, and the fear returns. It has become endemic. The circumstance itself is only one part of the problem; it is in our reaction to the circumstance that we break down. Like all forms of conditioning, liberation from fear is best attained through individual work with an experienced coach.

Take the simple analogy of a novice skier who finds himself high on a mountain when the sun begins to go down. He looks down into the valley to see the resort village far below. "I'll never get down there without breaking a leg," he says, and reveals that his fear is nine out of ten on the Richter scale.

ONE FEAR AT A TIME

His ski coach points to a hut 100 meters below them. "How afraid would you be to go down there?" he asks and the skier says, "That's easy; only a two on the scale."

They meet at the hut and the coach repeats the process to the next short stop, and so on down the mountain. The mountain was not the problem; his reaction to it was. What the skier had done was to take on his shoulders all his fear for the whole mountain. The tension not only in his shoulders but in his whole body might indeed have been leg breaking. What the coach did was to help him to break the fear down into bite-sized chunks instead, and facilitate the successful digestion of each chunk, one at a time.

So it is in the world of work. Big fears are generally an accumulation of a lot of small ones. By focusing exclusively on one challenge at a time, the whole is addressed. Over time and with repeated success, the skier or the executive will develop the ability to overcome small steps with little fear, thereby gaining more confidence in his capacity to manage fear, and to take responsibility for whatever fear reaction he does have in each circumstance.

**Fear in the mind**

Another novice skier may have run a similar but different story in his mind, this time about the size of the disaster rather than the size of the mountain. "But if I fall, I will break my leg," he says, although this is most unlikely, but then he adds, "Then how would I get down the mountain?" and then "I will be stuck here and freeze to death." Or he might think, "If I break my leg, I will not be able to work, so I will lose my job, then I will not be able to pay the rent, so my wife will leave me, and then I will kill myself." People can build an internal federal case out of their negative fantasies. Like the other skier, this one is in the future and not in his experience of the now, and he accumulates stories in his head, all of which are possible, none of which is probable. As we take responsibility for our stories, we gain the ability to create more realistic ones. The more self-responsible we are, the more fearless we become.

**Fear in the body**

That skiing analogy is an illustration of how our minds increase our fears and how they may be addressed, but we can also deal with fear through the body. The ski coach could ask:

"How do you know you are afraid?"

"I can feel it."

"Where in your body do you feel it most?"

"In my shoulders, they are so tight and my breathing is short and shallow."

"How tight is your right shoulder on a one to ten scale?"

"Eight."

"And the left one?"

"Six."

"What is your breathing doing now?"

"It's getting deeper and slower."

"Your right shoulder now?"

"Oh, four."

"And the left?"

"I can't feel it any more. Let us ski down!"
This time the coach focused the skier's attention on awareness, body awareness in this case. Fully experiencing the here and now leaves no space for, and sweeps away, the skier's frenetic thoughts about the there and then. It is a simple message, but it takes practice to embed this as a natural and automatic process until exaggerated fear becomes a thing of the past, and one is left with appropriate fear as a warning or safety device, though fear is perhaps no longer the appropriate word for it.

In the world of work, business plans, long-term planning, goal setting, and the like are considered to be essential good practice; however, they also contain an element of lack of trust, or of fear. They are very much there and then too, not here and now. Some of the most effective people talk about trusting emergence in the now; that means being confident that one is able to respond appropriately to eventualities as they arise, and it reflects a higher state of maturity. It reduces the need for and dependence on business plans, goal setting, and the like. The very thought of dispensing with those security blankets is scary and irresponsible to some, but it builds our agility for coping with an unpredictable future. I will return to that in the next chapter.

SEMCO

There are a few companies that operate in an altogether different paradigm, one of trust. Semco in Brazil is such a company. Ricardo Semler inherited Semco, a large marine engineering business, from his father, who had been a benevolent dictator. Over the ensuing years he transformed the company. Here are two examples of his expression of trust.

There always had been metal detectors on the exit gates to prevent workers from stealing hand tools, but when Ricardo took over he had them removed against the advice of his co-directors, who feared more theft. Initially that happened, but within weeks the stealing reduced to virtually nothing. The workers were policing themselves. Once they felt trusted, they became trustworthy.

Another policy Ricardo introduced was having open company accounts to which all staff had access and from which they could ascertain what everyone was paid. He then invited an ever-increasing proportion of his staff to choose their own salary. By and large he accepted their requests and no one took advantage of the system.

Ricardo Semler had one big advantage: he did not have to answer to institutional shareholders. Most corporate leaders do, and they have to deal with their fear of the cost and the risk of embarking on radical changes that shareholders might not comprehend or support. It is a tough call and a long haul for a large organization to shift from fear to trust, but trust is a key ingredient of future success.

## THREE STAGES OF DEVELOPMENT

Later in this chapter I will return to the means of clearing the debris of conditioning and I illustrate other ways in which fear can be tackled, but first we need to break down and define inner development work in three simple stages.

Terms such as personal development, self-development, psychological development, personal growth, and even psychospiritual development mean different things to different people. I will therefore explain how I am using them here. I describe the basic level of clearing up conditioning and excess fear as house cleaning, the middle level I term personal growth, and the higher level I call transpersonal development.

The overlap and sequence of personal development will vary from person to person and according to the situation. The journey toward enlightened leadership is far from straightforward, it is challenging, and it takes time. The importance of coaching for assisting a potential leader with personal development is that each element of psychological change progresses through four distinct steps for which **awareness** and **responsibility** are key. For example, in order to shed any form of conditioning, or indeed any old habits, it is first necessary for the person to recognize that a certain attitude or behavior is occurring. This is awareness raising by coaching, and it may take some time, even several sessions. The second step is to accept that this is a conditioned response; awareness raising again, but a more persistent challenge if it involves working through denial. The third is for the person to become willing to let go of the attitude or behavior; this is where responsibility kicks in and that may require tougher coaching. The fourth is consciously letting go; this is responsibility again, but with action planning. This is the coaching route for many of the basic changes early in the developmental journey.

As we become more self-aware, we are able to be more aware of others. The reason for this is simple. We all see the world through colored glasses: our perspective of others is distorted by our own psychological history, which determines our beliefs, attitudes, and values.

AWARENESS OF OTHERS

For example, if I experienced physical violence at home as a child, I might grow up seeing the world as a dangerous place and everyone around me as a potential threat. Consequently when I start to drive, I am liable to drive aggressively. I will not see people as they really are as long as my glasses are colored by my history, my conditioning. This distortion may cause me to be either timid or aggressive toward others, as a means of self-protection.

Furthermore, if I carry such a history, I might come to work one day and get into a row with you. I will most likely blame you for causing it, because to me you are a threat like everyone else. I will see the row as stemming from your aggression, not my distortion. Only when I become aware of my distorted perspective can I compensate for it or change it. I have to liberate myself from the grip of my past experience. This leads to self-management, for only if I am aware of what I am doing, or how I am reacting to you, can I change my behavior. Being told about it has little impact, realizing it myself has a lot. So the depth of my self-awareness determines the accuracy of my awareness of others and my capacity to self-manage, and all three together determine the quality of my social skills.

Deconditioning is a huge subject that could fill a library. It can be achieved by coaching, and maintained by self-coaching and self-awareness. It has been suggested that our behavior is 80 percent reaction and 20 percent action by choice. The

CHALLENGING OUR BELIEFS AND ASSUMPTIONS

following three coaching questions could be used as a frequently repeated mantra:

- "Where does the impulse come from for this action, thought or feeling?"
- "Is it my choice or the voice of my parents, of society, of the priest, or from my cultural norms?"
- "Is this true or is it an assumption or a belief?"

Naturally, as we recognize conditioning we have the opportunity to choose whether to accept it or change it. If we don't recognize it, we remain a victim of it.

How true or how valid are the beliefs and assumptions that we take to be true? These are just a selection of common types of assumption, with my counter challenge to each in italics:

- If the business does not keep growing, we are failing. *Quality can be success too.*
- I am or my company is too small to have an impact on climate change. *We all can, and do.*
- The capitalist free market is the best system for the future. *If so, we're dead.*
- Greed, selfishness, envy, secrecy, and cruelty are just human nature. *Are they?*
- If we don't sell them arms, other countries or companies will. *Who will start?*
- When these nonrenewables run out, we will find more somewhere. *Where?*
- Banks and great corporations are respectable social institutions. *Since when?*
- I never have quite enough. More is always better. *For whom and at what cost?*
- It is okay to throw it away. *Where is away?*
- Loyalty to my family is paramount. *What if they commit a serious crime?*

The list is endless. I suggest that you take the time to recognize and list your own and question them.

The baggage of conditioning and questionable beliefs takes time to shed, but as each piece drops away the journey of life gets lighter. Carrying our parents on our backs, long after we have grown up and they are dead, is a burden we don't need. We seldom question social conditioning beliefs even though they may be well past their sell-by date. True values that lead to right livelihood emerge from within and are integral, not imposed.

Whereas personal development is a never-ending journey, any aspiring leader, or coach, who fully invests him or herself in the processes espoused in this book will be well ahead of the game. Both coaches and leaders have a lot of catching up to do.

SHEDDING THE
BAGGAGE

# 22
# The Qualities of Leadership

*Leaders for the future need to have values and vision*
*and to be authentic and agile, aligned and on purpose*

Leaders of the future should be obliged to embark on their own journey of personal development to earn the title leader, in my opinion. We live in a world that seeks, even expects, instant gratification, but leadership qualities come neither quickly nor cheaply.

This chapter emphasizes four essential qualities that are likely to be common to all leaders, and ones that are especially relevant to the current times. The first is values, by which I mean personal, not company values.

## VALUES

It is widely believed, especially by religious people, that values stem from religion and that without religion we would have no values. This idea is false, for there are plenty of people who have no religious conditioning in their background and may be agnostic, if not atheistic, but still display exemplary values. The deeper reality is that our true values reside within us and at the deepest level those values are universal.

In the lower strata of personal development, which is unfortunately where much of humanity is at present, people are only vaguely in touch with their inner values, although those values may suddenly come to the surface in response to a crisis. The rest of the time they are buried in layers of parental, social, and cultural conditioning.

The extent of corporate crime and just plain greed is confirmation that many of those in power lack sufficient maturity or psychological development to be aware of their deeper inner values, let alone lead lives guided by them. This is made worse by a business ethos that, if it does not oblige people to focus on the financial rather than the social or environmental scorecard, encourages them to play the game the rest are playing. Shareholders, the institutional ones in particular, expect and demand financial returns, not those measured in human terms.

That is the old game, the old mentality, which is no longer sustainable or acceptable to a growing number of more mature and values-driven people. These are the leaders of the future, the only ones we can afford to accept or vote for if we care about the survival of our children and grandchildren.

A well-trained transpersonal coach (see Part IV for more on transpersonal coaching) will be able to use a number of exercises to penetrate beyond the conscious mind to enable aspiring leaders to access their values and other vital qualities. A coaching exploration of past activities and passions will reveal a pattern that can then be further honed in precision and broadened in scope. I can perhaps best illustrate this from my own experience.

I actively embarked on my own journey of personal development in 1970 when I went to study leading-edge psychology in California. I learned that I first had to escape from the worst of my parental, social, and cultural conditioning before I could begin to discover myself and my values, and to explore deeper social issues with greater clarity than I had ever experienced before. My concern then shifted away from myself toward others, and I was not happy with what I now saw in the world that I had ignored before.

**A PERSONAL EXAMPLE**

I began by evangelizing about personal development without much success; few people had heard of it. Then I got involved with anti-Vietnam war activism and moved on to concern about inequity and deprivation anywhere, and before long I was being drawn into so many issues. By this time I was clearly values driven, but I was far too scattered. With the help of a therapist, since coaching did not exist then, I discovered that the issues over which I was able to have some influence and the ones I was most passionate about were all related to justice. I cared about many other things, and was always supportive of others dealing with them, but it became clear that social justice was my path. I explored my subconscious to see if this was a therapeutic issue in the sense that I had, at some time in my distant past, suffered or caused some injustice and was trying to redeem myself. There was nothing there, so I began to accept that my purpose was to promote justice whenever possible.

Over time it became obvious that this was also too general and I needed to be more specific, so again, with the help of a coach by this time, I looked at the characteristics of all those things that I had become most frustrated by and most committed to changing. I discovered that the form of injustice I abhorred most was the abuse of power all the way from the micro to the macro, from child abuse to large companies' abuse of their staff, customers, and suppliers. This gave me real clarity about how and why I was attracted to coaching and leadership in big corporations. More macro still and most abhorrent of all to me is the abuse of small countries by superpowers and their power elite, their leaders.

I hope that this brief personal revelation illustrates the type of steps that can be taken if we choose first to become values driven and then to zero in on those values, which in turn can guide us to reset the sails of our lifeboat.

## VALUES-DRIVEN LEADERS

So we need leaders who are values driven – that means collective values not selfish values – and who are specific about their values so they can put them to best use for the most suitable issues. If a corporate executive doing what corporate executives do suddenly has a wake-up call, a heart murmur for example or a growing feeling of purposelessness, he might want to explore his values with a coach. The question may well arise of whether his personal values are sufficiently aligned with the corporate values; by that I mean the ones the company lives, not the ones it shouts about. If they are not, he is faced with some tough choices: to quit, to take responsibility to change the existing corporate values to be more aligned with universal higher values, or, if he is less senior, to find how he can still express his own values within the corporation to the benefit of all.

Richard Barrett, who used to work in HR for the World Bank, has devised what he calls corporate transformation tools, based on a model similar to Maslow's, to measure the values of everyone in a corporation. All the employees have to do is spend 15 minutes online to select from a template, customized for the specific company, a set of values that they hold, another set that represent how they see the existing corporate values, and a third set indicating the values they would like the corporation to have. The results are computer processed to give each person their own values sheet, together with a compilation of how staff see the company and how they would like it to be. The differences between the two show precisely where work needs to be done.

Smaller slices can also be extracted to show the values present by department, pay grade, gender, age, function, and so on, so that weaknesses in selected areas can be identified. The process provides a lot more valuable information than I can describe here, including a special section on leadership, but all that is available on the web or in Richard's books (see Bibliography). It is an outstanding system that I commend to all corporate coaches and human resource professionals when the board or the finance director in particular does not think internal policies and processes need to change. The findings are clear, stark, revealing, and persuasive in most cases.

However, if the directors, who are the ones who usually draw up corporate mission and values statements, find that they want to go one way and the staff call for another, they have a dilemma. Forcing staff to change their deeper values to align with the prescribed ones is likely to be disastrous. The directors will need to consider how they can better align the corporate values with those of their staff. That is indeed a switch of responsibility. In practice, compromises that meet everyone's needs can usually be found or negotiated.

## VISION

There is not much use in having values if they are not inclusive. By that I mean that if I value justice, I promote justice to all, not just to corporate clients and staff but to suppliers, citizens, the planet, and future generations as well. So the second quality that new leaders must have is an all-inclusive vision. They must discover and take account of their impact everywhere and change if necessary, placing impact ahead of cost in decision making at all times.

Because of increasing competition and uncertainty, business leaders easily become fixated on the bottom line. It is as if they become blinded by watching the numbers and are unable to raise their eyes to look beyond their computer screen, let alone out of the window to the world outside. How many leaders consider the impact of their decisions on future generations? Does that decision reflect and perpetuate old ways and therefore more environmental degradation or social injustice, or does it change things for good? Often they don't want to think about that; if they do, they are reminded that for them share value overrides higher values.

It is a no-brainer to say that leaders should have long-term vision if only in the financial sense, but in the world of the revolving door at the top and a big bonus each time you pass "Go," leaders are often chosen for their ability to deliver an immediate financial result, not for their vision. Long-term vision has been downgraded and devalued as a leadership quality, with potentially far worse consequences.

Vision in the past was largely narrow and focused, despite the fact that innovation and breakthroughs invariably come from a different or broader perspective on an issue. Today's world is so interconnected and communication so instant that whole-system thinking is already necessary, and it will be essential tomorrow. This emerges automatically as a product of the further reaches of personal growth.

Whole-system thinking relates strongly to values, in the sense that any and every action may lead to unexpected consequences in areas that appear unconnected. Since such eventualities are often totally unpredictable, doing the best under the circumstances means that every action one takes need to come from the highest of personal values. This in turn is a reflection of our purpose if we have traveled far enough along the journey of personal growth. Vision, values, purpose, personal growth, and much else besides are inextricably interconnected.

## AUTHENTICITY

The next essential leadership quality is authenticity: being who we really are, and not being afraid to be so in front of others. To achieve authenticity is an endless journey. It is about freeing ourselves from parental, social, and cultural conditioning, and also the false beliefs and assumptions we have accumulated along the way. It is also about freeing ourselves from fear: fear of failure, fear of being different, fear of looking stupid, fear of what others might think, fear of being rejected, and many more egocentric fears. The skiing analogy in the previous chapter provides some pointers on how coaching might work with all such fears.

The subpersonality model, described more fully in Chapter 24, can be very useful for coaches addressing authenticity issues. One stage further in personal growth is to learn, with the help of a transpersonal coach, to step back and become a dispassionate observer. This is a similar role to the conductor of an orchestra, who can call up any instrument or group of instruments and manage the whole symphony, but without playing a note himself. This is what we might describe as a state of self-mastery, and it brings with it a great deal of personal power and self-belief.

In psychosynthesis terms (see Chapter 24), this place is known as the "I," sometimes described as who we really are or our authentic self. Roberto Assagioli's definition of the "I" was a place inside of pure consciousness (**awareness**) and pure will (**responsibility**). This is the ideal state for a true leader to be in most of the time. It is a very powerful, fearless, authentic, consistent state that few people attain without being deeply invested in their own development. It equates with the top level of leadership, described in Jim Collins' book *Good to Great*, the principal qualities of level five being personal humility (self-awareness) and professional will (collective responsibility).

Perhaps it is now clear what lies beneath the task of any quality coach, which is to raise the coachee's **awareness** and **responsibility** at all times. Every time the coach helps the coachee to meet a small challenge, by being more aware and responsible for it, he is at the same time helping her to become more familiar with expressing the qualities of her "I"; in other words to draw closer to living from her "I" more regularly, or being more authentic more of the time.

The sort of transformation I write about here does not occur overnight or in a couple of coaching sessions. It is the product of commitment and persistence, and perhaps the odd "dark night of the soul," but this is a small price to pay for the benefits of being your "I" or who you really are much of the time. That is the place from which to lead others. It is absolute authenticity, and it stands alongside the best of values and vision.

## AGILITY

Another leadership quality I wish to emphasize is agility. The ability to be flexible, to change, to innovate, and to give up old beloved programs and goals is essential given the uncertain circumstances and speed of change in today's world. The willingness to change direction quickly when new conditions so demand may well become a survival necessity in the future. Agility is the product of two areas of personal growth work, to which I have already referred at some length. They are ridding oneself of the straitjacket of parental, social, and cultural conditioning and old beliefs and assumptions, and of eliminating fear, particularly the fear of the unknown that prevents people from being open to change. The unknown compasses many things, like uncharted waters, unforeseen reactions from others, and unexpected consequences in whole systems.

The term agility conjures up images of youthfulness and physicality. It is a widely held belief, and to some extent a reality, that we become less agile as we get older. How we perceive age in our mind can profoundly affect our physical and mental agility. I mentally gave up aging when I reached "retirement age" at 65, and the result of that is that I have a new and revitalized life. Recently I gave up jet lag.

It is a matter of personal choice, call it the placebo effect if you like. A positive attitude leading to a fair dose of self-belief reinforced by a good workout in the gym may not have much direct physiological impact, but it can act as a more powerful placebo than any pharmaceutical cocktail. Every muscle or joint in our body needs to be exercised if it is to remain pliable, and the same is true of our mind. As we get older, usually starting at about 30, we fall into countless small habit patterns. The same holiday location, the same wine, the same shopping day, the same clothes, the same walks or route to work, the same order in the same restaurant, the same phrases, the same reactions are all examples and causes of ossification.

Here is some agility homework. For one week at first – watch out, for it may later become a habit – each day try to avoid repetition in every little thing you do, from the smallest to the greatest. Make a list of all the things you still did habitually during the week and change them the following week. Greet people with the truth rather than a gratuitous platitude, ask the taxi driver about his interests, go and visit people in an old people's home, pick up rubbish in the hedgerow, talk to the busking musician or the street beggar and give £5 instead of 50p.

I was sitting outside a café in a square in Seville, Spain, having a coffee with my partner, and a busker was wandering round the outside of the group of tables playing his guitar. He then came back among the tables with his hat. My partner said

"No" to him and I felt instantly embarrassed. Then she said, "You were not playing for us. Will you play something just for us?" He was delighted and agreed. He asked what she would like him to play, and she replied, "I want you to play your favorite tune, the one that you would most like to play if you were alone on a beach or at home with your family." What and how he played was magnificent, of a totally different order to what he had been playing before. We all ended up in tears of joy; and he got well paid. Later a beggar conned me in the street and my partner, who is also my coach, persuaded me to go back and beg from the beggar. Think of a food that you would never order, and eat it anyway.

Just do something different, try it. In this way you are exercising your mental agility and probably your body as well. You will find out that you can survive when you do things differently. After all, habits are the safe repetition of fear-avoidance behavior. Breaking habits gives access to new avenues, makes life more interesting, opens the door to new discoveries, introduces new friends, makes you a far more interesting person, and may even give you tears of joy.

Some people may find it easier to experiment with such changes outside the workplace at first, but just the same principles can be applied at work. Agility is a life issue and one that we will increasingly need. Leadership is leadership and you can lead anything, just as coaching is coaching and you can coach anyone. This is the agility that is needed for the future.

## ALIGNMENT

Alignment in business is usually assumed to mean the alignment necessary between the members of the board or of a work team for the achievement of a goal or an agreed way of working. This type of alignment is indeed important, but even more important is the inner or psychological alignment within leaders themselves, without which the more common, outer form of workplace alignment is hard to achieve. So what is inner alignment?

THE QUALITIES OF LEADERSHIP    195

It is, of course, the alignment and collaboration between our subpersonalities, described in Chapter 24. If a business leader experiences an inner conflict over a major decision, the consequences can be far reaching. For example, one option might result in personal gain for the decision maker, such as can be the case in an acquisition or a demutualization. Another option might offer him less personal benefit but provide better long-term benefits for the business and its customers; a third option might be healthier for the community, for society, and for the environment.

Until he clearly resolves the inner conflict, he will not be fully committed even to the option he chooses. The choice he makes will depend on what he values most, or simply on his values. When different parts of ourselves, or subpersonalities, hold differing values, decision making becomes an internal battle of values for dominance. Since what we value changes, or rather expands, as we develop psychologically, this inner conflict is a natural consequence of our maturation process.

When team members have different objectives, the team will not be nearly as efficient or effective as it would be if they were aligned. However, the news is not all bad. Different views in a team can engender a healthy debate and a well-considered result that embraces several perspectives. Nevertheless, once the debate is over, everyone needs to be committed to the agreed decision. So it is with individuals, or should I say within individuals. Anyone who aspires to be a leader needs to develop his inner alignment. If he does not, others will experience him as somewhat schizophrenic and they will not know where they stand with him – they will not know who they are dealing with.

Sometimes the cause and extent of a leader's lack of alignment will not be consciously identifiable by him or by others; to them he will just seem inconsistent, unreliable, untrustworthy, or inauthentic. We do not have to look far among the current crop of corporate and political leaders to see how apparent and widespread that problem is. It is not surprising really, because we all have this problem to a greater or lesser degree. It is a part of the human condition, though it could be mitigated considerably in the parenting, education, and skill training process, were it more widely recognized and accepted.

## PURPOSE

What are we aligned toward, and for what purpose and for whose benefit? These are vital questions for leaders that remain to be answered.

I am being neither romantic nor elitist when I claim that we are at what is perhaps the most crucial time in all of human history. For the first time ever we have the capability to meet the basic needs of everyone on the planet, in terms of food, water, shelter, health, and education; and at the very same time, we have gained the capability to totally destroy our habitat and life as we know it.

We face a challenge and a choice – the ultimate choice between life and death on a macro scale. The challenge for many is to recognize it at all, and the choice is between doing the right thing or the short-term selfish thing.

Is it reasonable to suggest, therefore, that our individual purpose is a bit part in the whole universal purpose? Presumably our individual purpose can change as an effect of the changing human condition, and presumably also we can manifest our purpose wherever we find ourselves. It is hard to argue that business leaders and politicians should focus on any overall purpose or objective other than those that contribute to the sustainability of our habitat and of life on earth. How urgent do important issues have to become, for people to act – and then act in concert?

Forty years ago, before there was any widespread recognition or hard evidence of environmental degradation, resource shortage, and social unrest, a business leader might have been expected simply to go about his business. A young entrepreneurial leader would compete aggressively and be innovative and ambitious in his current trade while in parallel preparing himself for a greater leadership role in the future. He would tread on a few toes on the way, but generally be admired for climbing the ladder.

Another, perhaps more mature leader would grow his business, improve his products or services, look after his staff and his customers well, and contribute within his community. And then there are the so-called greats of yesteryear, highly successful at their own game of building huge multinational corporations of which they themselves were the outstanding beneficiaries, but they added little to the sum of human happiness, and occasionally they fell. All these would have been considered good, if not great, leaders until only a decade or so ago.

The context of leadership has changed dramatically for two reasons in particular. One is that many of the old rules and skills of leadership are no longer relevant to today's social conditions and entirely new ones are urgently needed. The other is that responsible leadership now demands that leaders make global, social, and environmental issues a priority on a par with, if not ahead of, the short-term financial success of their organization. If they do this, they can role model being responsible leaders and they will be as well prepared as they can be to lead their organization through the uncertain future.

## LEADERS FOR THE FUTURE

So leaders for the future need to have values and vision and to be authentic and agile, aligned and on purpose. Add awareness and responsibility to the mix, self-belief, and a good measure of emotional intelligence, and we have a powerful recipe. All these ingredients are organic, home grown, and carbon neutral for nothing is imported, in fact they are already just where you are and waiting to be harvested. In the final part of the book I look at the kind of coaching that can help us create and encourage such leaders.

# Part IV

# Transformation through Transpersonal Coaching

# 23
# Emotional Intelligence

*Emotional intelligence is twice as important as mental acuity for success in the workplace*

Maslow contributed more than just his hierarchy (described in Chapter 13) – along with Carl Rogers he was one of the founders of humanistic psychology, sometimes known as the third force of psychology that emerged after psychoanalysis, behaviorism, and cognitive psychology. Instead of studying mental illness and pathology as others had done before, Maslow studied healthy, fully functioning people to gain a deeper insight into human nature. The goal of humanistic psychology was the fulfillment of human potential through self-awareness, and it valued the emotions. It spawned many new experiential forms of psychotherapy and penetrated the business world in a limited way in the 1970s. It influenced the trend toward personal development, although it was not until 1995 that Daniel Goleman's book made emotional intelligence not only acceptable but desirable to the point of necessity in business. Goleman's research indicated that emotional intelligence (EQ) was twice as important as mental acuity (IQ) for success in the workplace. Everyone began to want some. It is a prerequisite for a professional coach.

Emotional intelligence is in fact nothing new, though the term is. It can be described as interpersonal intelligence or, even more simply, as social skills. This can be divided into five domains: knowing one's emotions (self-awareness), managing one's emotions, motivating oneself, recognizing emotions in others, and handling relationships. That sounds straightforward enough and we all combine these skills to some degree. Emotionally intelligent people just embody them more fully than others.

Goleman's research indicated that emotional intelligence is twice as important (66 percent to 34 percent) as academic or technical knowledge for success at work, for everyone not just leaders, both in terms of relationships and productivity. For leadership roles the ratio is even greater (85 percent to 15 percent).

On coach training programs I ask participants to recall an adult from their childhood, not a parent but someone they remember with particular affection. It may have been a grandmother or an uncle, or a friend of the family. I then ask them to list the characteristics that person had that made them so much more memorable than all the other adults. I get the participants to compare notes and they are amazed at the consistency and commonality of those characteristics – and this remains true regardless of country or culture.

Those qualities look something like this:

- They treated me as if I was an equal to them.
- They listened to me and were interested in my opinion.
- They gave me their full time and attention.
- They challenged me.
- They believed in me; they believed that I could.
- They were fun, enthusiastic, and made me laugh.
- I felt cared for, loved, supported, and safe with them.
- They respected me.

I then ask the group how they felt when they were with this person and their answers are equally consistent: special, valued, confident, and, most frequently, self-belief.

Of course there are other responses too, but these are the most consistent. Becoming more emotionally intelligent or choosing appropriate behaviors is not about checking a list of your behaviors against an academic ideal. It is much simpler simply to imagine your special older person and compare yourself with what she would do under this or that circumstance. She had loads of emotional intelligence – use her as a role model.

If emotional intelligence is so important for success at work, and school is supposed to prepare children for life, it is an inexcusable omission that schools do not include classes in it. The assumption is, of course, that such social skills are learned through social interaction with peers and adults, and that they cannot or need not be taught. This is erroneous on both counts. In fact school would provide an ideal environment for developing the emotional intelligence of young people, through play, structured interactive exercises, and coaching.

No sooner had we digested EI or EQ, abbreviations by which emotional intelligence became known, than several new books appeared advocating the merits of SQ or spiritual intelligence. Spiritual in this sense is not a religious concept but is defined by author Elisabeth Denton as "the basic desire to find ultimate meaning and purpose in one's life and to live an integrated life." In her book *Spiritual Intelligence*, Danah Zohar quotes a 36 year-old businessman describing his personal crisis:

*I am managing a large and successful company here in Sweden. I have good health; I have a wonderful family, a position in the community. I suppose I have "power." But still I am not certain what I am doing with my life. I am not certain I am on the right path doing the job that I do.*

He explained that he was very worried about the state of the world, especially the condition of the global environment and the breakdown of the community. He felt people were avoiding the real scale of the problems facing them. Big

SPIRITUAL
INTELLIGENCE

businesses like his were especially guilty of not addressing such problems. "I want to do something about it," he continued. "I want, if you like, to use my life to serve, but I don't know how. I just know that I want to be part of the solution. Not the problem."

So how does a coach work with such issues, and what skills does he or she need? Certainly to be most effective coaches do need to go beyond the basic skill level of asking questions to raise **awareness** and **responsibility**, listening well, running with the coachee's agenda, and following the GROW sequence. There is much more to coaching than that, and this takes us into the next evolution of psychology.

24

# Tools of Transpersonal Psychology

*Much of the psychological dysfunction in the world stems from frustration about the lack of meaning and purpose in our lives*

Many years ago I was drawn to the depth and inclusiveness of psychosynthesis, a whole-system perspective of psychology, and it has informed my coaching work ever since. Psychosynthesis was conceived by Dr. Roberto Assagioli in 1911. He had been a student of Freud and was the first Freudian psychoanalyst in Italy. Like Carl Jung, his friend and fellow student, he rebelled against Freud's limited pathological and animalistic vision of man. Both suggested that humans possess a higher nature and Assagioli asserted that much of the psychological dysfunction in the world stems from frustration or even desperation about the lack of meaning and purpose in our lives.

Assagioli was far ahead of his time and psychosynthesis remained relatively obscure until the 1960s, when it became a primary component of the emerging fourth force of psychology known as transpersonal psychology. It does not replace the third force (humanistic psychology) but embraces and builds on it. It adds a deeper sense of the will, the experience of meaning, purpose, and direction, personal responsibility, and placing others before self – all based on the hypothesis that each of us has a deeper identity or a higher organizing principle. We could claim, and I do, that purpose is transpersonal, and meaning is humanistic.

Psychosynthesis offers a number of maps and models, the strands of which weave a very useful cradle for in-depth coaching. One of these is a simplified model of human development that, like all models, is not the truth but merely a representation that enables a conversation to take place with a coach or within our own minds. A psychosynthesis-trained coach will invite the coachee to reframe life as a developmental journey, to see the creative potential within each problem, to see obstacles as stepping stones, and to imagine that we all have a purpose in life with challenges and obstacles to overcome in order to fulfill that purpose. The coach's questions will seek the coachee's recognition of the positive potential in the issue and the actions he chooses to take.

## TWO DIMENSIONS OF GROWTH

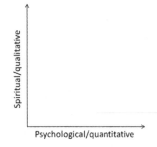

We can trace our experience of our own life track or that of others on a two-dimensional graphical model, of which the horizontal axis represents material success and psychological integration and the vertical axis represents values or spiritual aspiration. Here is an example of two very different types of people to illustrate the two axes.

A business person may be focused on personal achievement and success in the material world and may have become a well-integrated person, a good parent, and a respected member of society, without ever having asked themselves a meaningful question about life. This is the tendency of western people, which has resulted in great material progress and innovation. The business person might regard the opposite type, the one that follows, as lazy, disorganized, a sponger, a dilettante.

Actually this is the mystical type who leads a contemplative and ascetic life, but who seems ill-equipped to cope with the realities and essentials of the everyday world. Their home, their finances, and even their personality may be in a bit of a mess. These people live a monastic life of study or art, and readily give gentle assistance to others. They see the business person's pursuits as being pointless, ego driven, and often destructive to themselves and to others. This is the more eastern path; although given the economic growth of the East of late, these geographic distinctions are liable to be confusing, or even contradictory.

There can be little argument that western people have focused their energies on moving along the horizontal axis and have done so with gusto and to good effect. Western influence and economic imperatives have long been a pervasive global force but, in both East and West, there are many who journey up the vertical axis. The further we progress along either path to the exclusion of the other, the more we depart from the ideal or balanced path between the two and the tension thereby created increases.

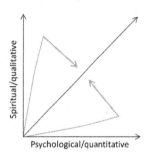

If social pressures, business imperatives, or blind determination to achieve override the tension that is attempting to pull us back on track, we are liable eventually to run into a wake-up wall. This wall is known as the crisis of meaning. When we hit the crisis wall, we tend to bounce back in shock into temporary confusion and even performance regression for a while, but at the same time we are likely eventually to be pulled upward toward the ideal to discover a more balanced path. We may become more introspective, paint or write poetry, and want to spend more quality time with the kids.

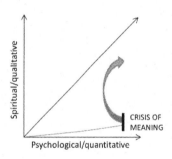

The horizontal axis can also be equated to knowledge. The crisis of meaning occurs when our accumulation of knowledge far exceeds the tempering effect of our values. In the crisis we experience a breakdown of the false sense of security provided by the illusion of power and certainty that great knowledge gives us.

KNOWLEDGE

Wisdom lies beyond knowledge and is deeper. It provides foresight, it is often paradoxical, and it offers a different order of security that a person emerging from the crisis is then able to experience. The 45° line in the diagrams could thus be said to represent wisdom, lying between the extremes of what we might cynically describe as indiscriminately exploited knowledge on one side and ungrounded spiritual fanaticism on the other. Vertical excess can also lead people to a crisis, known as the crisis of duality, the split between their idealistic vision and the harsh realities of mundane life. They are brought down to earth with a bump, and may find themselves compromising their values to get a proper job.

## CRISIS MANAGEMENT

Could humanity right now be in the throes of a collective global crisis of meaning? Knowledge is often said to be the valued currency of today and the future. For centuries humanity presided over a land-based economy, then with the Industrial Revolution came a shift to a capital-based one. Landowning aristocrats gave way to nouveau riche merchants. In the knowledge-based economy the technophiles may appear to hold sway, but their grip has been proved to be tenuous and they have a long way to fall. Is this an indication that the gap between our knowledge and our wisdom is too great to be sustainable? Certainly it has been the main contributor to the unsustainability of our environment and the fragility of our economy. Could we now be glimpsing the emergence of the next phase, the wisdom-based economy? Can we hope that the politicians and business leaders of the future will be truly wise, or should we rather be looking for wisdom within ourselves, finding our own inner leadership? Or does the economic crisis have to run its course?

I have omitted one element from the psychosynthesis diagrams above, a point of light that lies beyond the 45° arrowhead. It represents our higher self or soul, which could be seen as the source of our purpose and of wisdom. It exerts a gentle pull on us to "get back on track," one that is easily overridden by our more earthbound desires and ambitions. In the past such a notion could easily be dismissed by rational scientific minds as fanciful speculation. However, recent advances in neurobiology have revealed what is called the

"God spot" in the temporal lobes of the brain that, to quote Danah Zohar, could be "a crucial component of our larger spiritual intelligence."

Business rightly recognizes that many systems in the world are shifting from push to pull, from prescription to choice. This can be described as the shift from the push for success to the pull from the soul. Pulling what we want off the internet is superseding our blind acceptance of the junk mail *they* want to push on to us. A coach pulls out of the coachee his own inner knowing rather than pushing onto him what he should do. A coaching management style does the same. People want and will continue to expect more personal choice in the future.

Of course, a crisis is not a prerequisite for psychospiritual development. Some people travel far along their journey with neither a crisis nor a coach. Others progress with less dramatic consequences through a series of mini-crises and the direction changes are not as acute. To coach such a person, good basic coaching training will generally be adequate. In fact under almost all circumstances, if a coach sticks tightly to non-prescriptive principles and follows the coachee's agenda, little will go wrong.

The problem arises when a coach, unaccustomed to and therefore alarmed by extreme outbursts and sudden swings of emotion, panics and intervenes to try to help the person to control their feelings. The coach has reverted to his own self-protecting agenda. The coachee usually needs to enter into and, if necessary, relive residual suppressed emotions at his own pace, albeit with process guidance, support, and protection from the coach.

Coaching someone through a crisis of meaning is seldom a one-stop intervention; a series of sessions over a period of several months is likely to be required. Furthermore the coach needs to be prepared for different outcomes; for example, after his company has invested money and time in his in-depth coaching, the coachee may nevertheless decide to leave his job and find alternative work more in tune with his newly identified and clarified purpose.

## COACHING FOR A CRISIS

I will not go into more detail here about all the techniques and potential pitfalls of coaching people through a major crisis of meaning once it happens. It can be a profound experience and an unsettling time for people who have traveled a long way along the horizontal plane before it occurs. I strongly advocate some training in psychosynthesis or a similar psychology for independent coaches who wish to enter this field or may unexpectedly find themselves there. It is a specialist area that is likely to be beyond the brief time availability, experience, or capability of what we might describe as a conventional coach.

In-depth coaching is an invaluable resource for helping people to clear away their defensive shields and self-imposed blockages, so that they can more readily experience their own inner guidance. Hearing and obeying the "still small voice within" early enough may be a good way to avert a crisis and coaching can certainly contribute to that, and help us to stay on purpose. Unfortunately, all too often people do not seek that coaching help and support until they have hit the wall. It might also be tempting for some businesses to keep their head in the corporate sand as a way out of the complexities of meaning and purpose. In the long run, however, I believe that those businesses that stand by their people in their hour of need will have that goodwill returned many times over.

To cover the full range of models, techniques, skills, and benefits of transpersonal skills is beyond the scope of this book. Transpersonal psychology has many therapeutic and other applications beyond coaching, but I will focus on a key model here and provide a taster of a number of others that lend themselves especially well to coaching.

## SUBPERSONALITIES

*There are times when I look over the various parts of my character with perplexity. I recognize that I am made up of several persons and that the person that at the moment has the upper hand will inevitably give place to another. (Somerset Maugham)*

This model works with what we call subpersonalities, different aspects of ourselves that may have different characteristics and objectives. For example, have you ever woken up some bright, sunny morning and thought, "Wow, why don't I get up and go for a walk on the beach?" and within an instant you hear another inner voice countering, "No, relax, stay in bed; it's so warm and comfortable here"? Who is talking to whom? These are two of your subpersonalities and you have many more, including the one that listened to both sides of the dialog. We all know someone who puts on his business suit, admires himself in a mirror, and walks, shoulders back and upright, to the office. Is that how he walks and talks when he is out with his mates, or visiting his grandmother, or with the kids? Probably not.

We all adopt certain characteristics, even personalities, in different circumstances depending on how we see ourselves or want to be seen. Have you ever walked a little more bow-legged after watching a cowboy film? Many subpersonalities stem from our childhood when we subconsciously, in part anyway, used a strategy to get what we wanted from a parent. "Can I have another chocolate please – oh pleeeese!" with the high voice, the bowed head, and the poor-me stance to match. If that strategy does not work, we try another until we succeed, then we refine it. We find it works with other people too, and into our adulthood, and not only for chocolate. Most subpersonalities have a need and many have a gift too – for example the Hero is likely to be courageous, a useful gift if someone needs to be saved.

A coach would be ill-advised to dive in with a client by explaining the theory of subpersonalities and asking him to list their own. Instead, when a client has an inner conflict of some sort, one can ask, "What part of you wants to do that?" and then "What other characteristics does that part have? What does the other part want?" The purpose of the coaching questions is to help the coachee to recognize and understand more about his drives and his inner conflicts as a prelude to resolving them. When the client is comfortable with you, you

## COACHING FOR AN INNER CONFLICT

should be able to ask him to list some names (Chocoholic, Hero, Victim, and so on) for his own subpersonalities.

Many coaching questions evolve from that point:

* Which one of these do you find most disruptive?
* Under what circumstances does this one show up?
* Give me an example of a recent time.
* What did it want at that time?
* Did it get it? And if so how do you think the other person felt?
* What would be another way of getting what you want in those circumstances?

The client's self-awareness is being increased by this process to the point that he can begin to make choices about how he presents himself instead of going into a certain subpersonality automatically because of the circumstances. His self-responsibility is being strengthened and he is moving toward a greater sense of self-mastery. When two subpersonalities are in conflict with each other (e.g., walking on the beach) – and that will often be a repetitive pattern – it is possible to invite the coachee to conduct an imaginary conversation between the two parts and even have them negotiate (e.g., walk three times a week and stay in bed four days).

## WHO ARE YOU?

One way of describing our subpersonalities is to recognize that we "identify" with certain descriptions, roles, and even objects. If you ask a stranger "Who are you?" she will usually give you her name. But if people are gathering to help or gawp at an accident, a police officer or a relative might ask someone pushing through the crowd "Who are you?" In this circumstance the person may say "I am a doctor," for that is more relevant than her name. Under various circumstances people will see and describe themselves as a business person, an Arsenal supporter, an accountant, a racing driver, a feminist, an American, a mother, a school teacher, an academic; you name it. None of those things is really who they are, but they are the part of themselves that they are identified with at that moment or under those circumstances.

Some people get severely stuck in one subpersonality, thereby denying their own access to other parts of themselves that may be more interesting, creative, humorous, appropriate, and so on. Some even get identified with objects, like their clothes or their car; they don't just *have* them, they *become* them. It is important that people get to discover who they are behind these temporary and superficial identifications.

A person can be likened to a team in which the different members have different qualities and different wishes and expectations. It is important to get the team to be open with each other, talk about their needs and differences, and start to collaborate and even support each other in order to meet their individual aspirations. Coaching can help a person to become much more integrated and consistent in themselves and with other people. You will notice that this process is a matter of raising self-**awareness** and then self-**responsibility**.

In the workplace, and indeed at home too, a great deal of conflict comes from one subpersonality of one person locking horns with one subpersonality of another and that becomes all consuming. Once they are aware that it is only a part of one person in conflict with a part of the other, the energy in the conflict is defused, both can start to manage their subpersonalities and can adopt a different one with each other, and they may even find themselves in agreement about things they previously fought over.

Subpersonalities can be used in many ways and they appear in many forms. Even teams can be viewed as having subpersonalities. Another useful analogy is that the subpersonalities are members of a symphony orchestra: each plays a different instrument, but they can be grouped. When they tune up before the concert each makes their own sound and the uncoordinated noise heard outside is far from pleasant. Then, however, the conductor appears, and in an instant he has the orchestra playing in harmony.

SELF-MASTERY

This raises the next question, "Can I become the conductor of my own orchestra?" The answer is yes, by disidentifying or stepping back from your subpersonalities and becoming the observer of the process. I hasten to add that this is quite deep stuff and it does not happen overnight, but being the conductor of your own orchestra is a very calm and powerful state that we call self-mastery. In psychosynthesis terms the conductor is known as the "I" and it is described as a center of pure consciousness and pure will. This equates precisely with **awareness** and **responsibility**, so you can now see that the core purpose of coaching is building the qualities and the presence of the "I." It is no coincidence that this also equates with the qualities of the leaders in the highest level of leadership identified by Jim Collins in his book *Good to Great*. They are humility, an inevitable partner of self-awareness, and will or passion.

So what is the sequence you need to follow to reach alignment, and do you need a coach?

- Step one is the recognition that you have subpersonalities at all, identifying your most active ones and when they take you over. This requires honest self-reflection of a kind that would benefit a lot from the assistance of a coach.
- Step two is the willingness to acknowledge to another or to others that conflicting subpersonalities exist and to discover when they show up and take you over, what they want, how they limit you, and how they may serve you.
- Step three is to get them to cooperate with one another, and this is where inner alignment starts. For example, going back to the story I told earlier about different voices advocating going for a morning run or staying in bed, the two voices could, in a role-play exercise, negotiate a compromise such as two early runs a week in exchange for three lie-in mornings without guilt.
- The fourth and final stage is one of true synthesis or collaboration to the same end for the good of the whole. While this kind of developmental process work can be undertaken at home through self-reflection, meditation, and visualization, the processes themselves need prior experience or training. It is probably best done with the help of a psychosynthesis-trained coach, and there are additional benefits of doing it in a training group designed for this express purpose.

## DEEPER UNDERSTANDING

At the deeper levels of coaching, the coachee will be gaining access to the subconscious mind where much of our pain and our potential lies untapped. The pain part is what Freud called the lower unconscious, analogous to the basement of the house, dank, dark, and with skeletons and spiders. That is not coaching territory – that is for therapists. The living quarters are known as the middle unconscious, though quite a proportion of this is conscious – our normal waking consciousness. With normal coaching we are effectively enlarging the percentage of the normal consciousness area. Transpersonal coaching opens the door to the superconscious realm that Assagioli equated with the balconies, the rooftop, and the sun beyond, and the reservoir of potential, of creativity, of innovation, of aspiration, of peak experience, the absolute of joy, love, and compassion. Helping a coachee to explore this realm and learn to go there at will is therefore the goal of the transpersonal coach. Let us now move from the house to the egg metaphor.

The egg is a psychosynthesis diagram (overleaf) that many find a helpful way of illustrating and understanding the positioning of and the relationship between the different parts of the human psyche.

- The outer shell of the egg represents the container of the person, but you will notice that the shell is a permeable dotted line, suggesting that human consciousness is not imprisoned therein.
- The darker lower unconscious is the basement of the person, with spiders, sex, and skeletons in the proverbial closet. It is our psychological past and where past damage may be retained. It is the province of Freud and psychotherapists, not coaches.
- The middle unconscious is readily accessible by good coaching. It is the more recent and the present time, and it is where the majority of workplace coaching takes place.
- The field of awareness represents the immediate waking day-to-day awareness, and most coaching is about

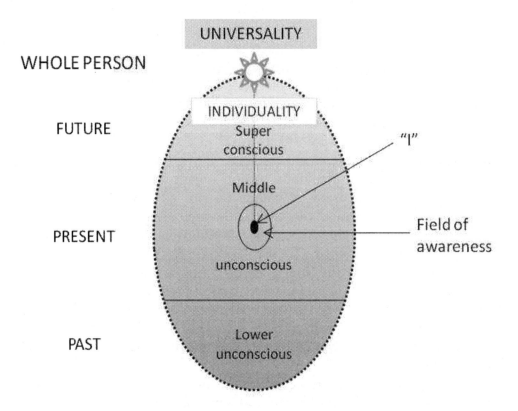

expanding this area to bring more of the middle unconscious into consciousness.

- The "I" is at the center of the field of awareness but it hides deep down, and needs to be surfaced.
- The superconscious is where our potential is stored, our joy, our aspiration, our creativity, our inspiration, and our peak experiences. This is what the transpersonal coach is skilled at opening up.
- Then top center is the self or the soul, which is both of the individual and of the universal at the same time. It is very rarely experienced but if it is momentarily, it is the glorious oneness of the universe.
- The dotted line connecting the "I" with the self is a bridge that when solidly built by deep transpersonal work connects the "I" to the self and enables the qualities and the purpose of the self to manifest through the "I." It

represents true alignment between the personal will and the universal will.

I have described the transpersonal realm here for the understanding of aspiring coaches. I strongly advise all interested coaches to attend a course or two on transpersonal coaching, because practice in a safe environment and getting feedback is crucial to learning. I hope the revelations about the transpersonal in these pages will encourage you to do so, but if you feel comfortable with trying out some of the principles and exercises described here with friends and colleagues, by all means do that. There is not one right way to do anything, but what follows shortly is a detailed description of the use of one form of transpersonal coaching, that you could, at first at least, follow quite closely.

## THE MOUNTAIN OF LIFE

Many transpersonal coaching methods seek to reach beneath the rational, logical, and limited mind into the subconscious, which is a whole system. For example, guided imagery can be used to have the coachee imagine himself on a journey up a mountain, an archetypal symbol for growth, suggest to him that he meets certain things on the way, from gifts to obstacles, from an animal to a wise old teacher, and ask him to imagine what happens when this occurs. The events that occur, the obstacles he finds, and the beings he meets on the way are all symbols of something in the coachee's mind that is uncovered during the subsequent coaching.

I give here the sort of script I use, although I recommend saying it unprepared and spontaneously when you are confident enough. It will sound more authentic.

• Just sit quietly and comfortably for a moment and take a few deep breaths.
• Now see yourself in a field surrounded by nature at the foot of a mountain.

- Begin to slowly walk toward the mountain, and start up the first gentle slope.
- As you go it begins to get steeper and more rugged.
- You are now in trees and there are rocks around you.
- All of a sudden you come upon an apparently insurmountable obstacle.
- You want to continue and you figure out how to overcome it.
- It may be a struggle, but eventually you make it and continue on your way.
- Unexpectedly you meet an animal, and more unexpectedly still, it speaks to you.
- Are you afraid? What does it say? Is it afraid? What do you say?
- It is time to continue your climb and you say goodbye.
- You come to the edge of the tree line and the clear mountain opens before you.
- There on the path is a gift that you know is for you. You pick it up and take it with you.
- Now you are approaching the top of the mountain and the view is magnificent.
- As you come round a piece of rock, there is a wise old person sitting there.
- He or she greets you and indicates that she was expecting you.
- She invites you to ask her three questions and she will give you the answers.
- You ask the questions that come to your mind one at a time and receive her answers.
- You let the answers sink in and she bids you farewell, and you begin to retrace your steps.
- The journey down the mountain is leisurely but it does not take very long.
- Soon you find yourself back in the field where you started.
- When you are ready, slowly come back to the room and open your eyes.

I then get the coachee to take a pen and pad and make notes of all he remembers, including the conversation with the animal and the questions he asked and the answers he received from the wise old person. When he has finished and after a breather, I coach him on the experience, focusing mainly on what the obstacle symbolized to him and what qualities he deployed to overcome it. What was the animal and his feelings about it? What was the conversation with it, and what did that symbolize? Next, what was the gift, who was it from, and what does it mean? And finally, who was the wise old person, what were the questions, what were the answers received, and, importantly, what did they tell you? There are, of course, many other aspects of the experience that might arise that need to be explored, but this gives you the gist.

In terms of timing, the mountain climb should be slow and deliberate, with enough time between each sentence, maybe around 20 seconds, with the whole journey up and down taking, say, 15 minutes. The debrief will be as long as a piece of string.

I hope this gives you enough of an idea of this sort of process to allow you to experiment with it. It is very important that you develop your own authentic style with this type of work.

## OTHER TRANSPERSONAL TOOLS

Here is a somewhat similar exercise. The client, or this can be done with a team all together, can be given sheets of paper and a variety of colored crayons, and asked to draw whatever comes to their consciousness in response to certain questions, no more than four. For example, "Where are you coming from?" "Where are you now?" "Where are you going?" "What qualities do you need to get there?" Again, the subsequent processing is where all the richness emerges.

The room should be in silence throughout. Give the questions one at a time and allow at least five minutes for each drawing, more if it feels right. The processing questions are again asking the coachees how they chose the colors and the shapes, what they represent, and what they say. If you are working with a team they may do the processing in pairs, but you need to give them the sort of questions they should be asking each other.

Another very simple and yet powerful exercise is to ask the client to recall a time when she really valued what she was doing; then a time when she was very passionate about what she was doing; and then a third question would be to ask what she does very well. Again, give the coachee plenty of time to dwell on each question one at a time, and to make notes if she wants to. A key question here is about the common elements of these scenarios and the common qualities that the coachee was expressing at those times. By increasing her self-awareness of all these elements, the client may form a clearer idea of what she would like to be doing and her purpose.

## FINDING OUT MORE

A sensitive coach should be able to use all of these tools judiciously with the right client and thereafter gain confidence, see the effects, and develop his own preferences and style, without going too deep at first. However, I highly recommend attending at least a two-day training course in transpersonal coaching, if at all possible. It will broaden your range of skills and foster your own personal development too.

Transpersonal coaching skills will be more and more in demand as time and collective psychosocial evolution progress and I am strongly recommending to the coaching establishment that the qualification criteria for all coaches include a section on the transpersonal.

If you wish to read more about the transpersonal and its use with yourself and others, the best book for this is by my ex-wife, Diana Whitmore, *Psychosynthesis Counselling in Action*.

# 25

# The Future Focus of Coaching

*We must take our responsibility, and help others to do the same;*
*we don't have all the answers, but we can help others to find theirs*

When I wrote the first edition of this book in 1992, it was one of the first books specifically on coaching and it has served to define coaching in many countries throughout Europe, Asia, the Pacific rim, and Latin America. Now there are a plethora of coaching books covering coaching from every angle and for every application. Many of them are excellent and they all add weight to the relevance, value, and standing of coaching. When we started Performance Consultants more than 20 years ago, we were one of the only purveyors of coaching in Europe; now there are upwards of 1,000 coaching businesses and more than 10,000 coaches in Europe involved in business, education, healthcare, charities, government departments, and every other activity imaginable. Doctorates and degrees in coaching are offered through a number of universities and business schools. There are a growing number of professional associations of coaching that are promoting standards and ethics, qualifications and certification. The largest of these is the International Coach Federation, which in 2008 had 15,000 members worldwide.

So the coaching profession is expanding fast and it has managed to avoid many of the pitfalls of burgeoning popular start-up initiatives. The cowboys who saw coaching as a means to a fast buck have largely failed because, with such motivation, they could not offer the standards of integrity that the profession demands. There are differences in the form of coaching offered: some are based on the earlier behavioral and cognitive psychologies; most are based on humanistic principles, recently relabeled positive psychology; and increasingly those are topping up with the next level, transpersonal psychology.

Humanistic coaching allows for the spiritual, transpersonal coaching embraces it. Behavioral and cognitive coaching deny it, and while they may be very usable in certain circumstances, they do not address the whole person, because the spiritual realm is an integral part of the whole. It is only in the materialist western culture that psychological development and spiritual development are separated, although the gap is closing fast.

While coaching is in good health, huge challenges lie ahead as people everywhere recognize their limitations and know that they have to change their way of thinking and being if their organization is to serve its purpose in an ever-changing world. More companies and leaders will recognize that they need personal growth and will seek coaches to facilitate their development, but the coaches themselves will also need to be up to scratch with their own development if they are to be of value. To be able to offer a full service, the standard of coaching skill must be raised to include psychological and spiritual understanding, personal development experience, transpersonal coach training, and a working knowledge of current global affairs. At this point coaches themselves become leaders, and leaders need to be coaches to bring out the best in those they lead. The roles and functions merge.

## COACHING IN NEW AREAS

What I have been seeing recently is large institutions changing their orientation toward coaching and a coaching management style. Here is an example. I have been co-opted onto a three-year European Commission project, the brief for which is to plan and recommend processes whereby the way road driving is taught throughout Europe is transformed from instruction to coaching. The rationale for this is that a disproportionate number of young male driver fatalities are the result of emotional mismanagement rather than technical inability. Coaching addresses that realm automatically; instruction does not touch it at all. There are half a million driving instructors in Europe, 40,000 in Britain alone, and 4,000 new ones coming on stream each year.

To take another sector, more and more concern is being expressed about healthcare and its inhuman technological bias. The family doctor's bedside manner, which used to be so healing, is being systemized and dehumanized. While the media berates the UK National Health Service, most people are very satisfied when asked about their personal experience of the NHS. The US health system, on the other hand, is a disgrace, with huge amounts of money spent and made in some quarters and the less well-off falling though the health net altogether. The US spends more on health per capita than any other country in the world by far and yet it is rated around twentieth in terms of the health quality it delivers. The whole system has been hijacked by the pharmaceutical and insurance industries between them to maximize profits rather than optimize health.

The health benefits of educating people and patients alike to take greater responsibility for their own health would be far greater than the pharma industry can deliver, and at a fraction of the cost. This is not a nanny state idea, it is in fact the opposite, getting people to take more care of themselves. This issue has some of the same coaching characteristics as the European driver education project. The need is for self-responsibility in both, and that is what coaching is committed to delivering.

In times of crisis, turmoil, and great change, normal skills training and personal development courses seem rather irrelevant. Coaching ex-bank executives on how to clear their desks and their consciences, or on career change, would seem to have better prospects, but many people at every level in our economic hierarchy suffer from uncertainty and insecurity.

## COACHING FOR CHANGE

They will ask questions that they thought they would never have to, and the politicians stumble to provide little more than short-term quick fixes. The most useful answers will be those that emerge from within each of us. We may not be able to stabilize the economy, but we can find personal stability within economic instability.

The coaching profession has a hugely significant role to play in times of crisis. It serves individuals through life coaching and the collective through corporate coaching. At the remedial end of the spectrum, coaches with some psychological and especially transpersonal skills can provide support and a stable grounding for those who are stressed and distressed by ever-changing and trying circumstances, especially if their concerns are for their children. Helping people to make sense of what is going on economically, environmentally, or in the event of social breakdown, for example, is very much the province of transpersonal coaches. While I recommend that all coaches gain some transpersonal skills, I do not imply here that people with basic coaching skills cannot do great work; indeed, emotional intelligence alone is already a considerable asset.

Coaches can help people to free themselves from the many fears that limit their ability to remain flexible and responsive enough to deal with fast-emerging and sometimes unexpected times. For some the ability to accept that things will never be quite the same again, or to let go of perceived essentials in terms of possessions, food, or habits, constitutes quite a challenge, one that is again rooted in fear. However, these are all relatively straightforward issues that are by no means limited to times of crisis. The more relevant point for coaches now is how much they need to know about wider issues and what they do with that knowledge.

I strongly recommend that anyone who professes to be a coach should be well informed about environmental and economic issues and trends, and should keep up to date with current affairs not only in their own country but globally. Armed with this knowledge, they should be better equipped to ask more precise coaching questions, and should be willing to be informative, if and when that is appropriate.

Information is not the same as prescription. Importantly, coaches should not hold an overly rosy or sycophantic view of political or corporate leaders, money men or media moguls, and other purveyors of power and spin.

When it comes to coaching business leaders, broad current general knowledge is vital, because coaches must be prepared to challenge the ethics, values, and behaviors of their coachee if necessary. I believe that coaches should maintain a higher set of ethics that ultimately takes precedence over the self-interest of the client or of the client company. I believe also that a coach should be willing to reject or drop a client on ethical grounds, even if that means losing a lucrative contract.

COACHING FOR PERSONAL GROWTH

Coaching is not a panacea to all ills in work, in life, or in the world, but it is infinitely more than a tool for helping stressed executives, or a better management method for use in a variety of situations such as planning, delegating, or problem solving. Coaching is one of the most acceptable skills for human growth. It is a different way of viewing people, a far more optimistic way than most of us are accustomed to, and it results in a different way of treating them. It requires us to suspend limiting beliefs about people, including ourselves, abandon old habits, and liberate ourselves from redundant ways of thinking.

I remain steadfastly optimistic about the future of coaching. It is undeniable that coaching, or the principles on which it is based, is becoming ever more widely recognized and used. We may drop the word coaching or add new terms to the crop that already exist: counseling, facilitating, empowering, mentoring, supporting, guiding, psychotherapy. Their applications differ somewhat but they overlap, and though they may be expressed differently, the underlying principles of **awareness** and **responsibility** are common to all and are at the very core of human growth and effectiveness.

The need for what coaching offers is everywhere and in every institution, every corporation, every school, and every social structure. Coaches are midwives at the birth of a new social order, one in which compassion for all people and caring for all of nature and our only home form the core theme. What more rewarding challenge could there be?

That sounds like a tall and grandiose order for the fledgling industry that coaching is, but I assert it with great humility. We coaches represent the principles of the new order and we are trained and well equipped to coach, guide, support, and heal those who will become more confused and anxious about the enormity of world events that will increasingly impinge on their lives and their hopes for the future. We must take our responsibility, and help others to do the same; we don't have all the answers, but we can help others to find theirs. This is how we can play our part in the transformation from hierarchy to self-responsibility, and a better world for all.

So does coaching have a future? What do you think?

# Appendix: Some solutions to the nine dot exercise

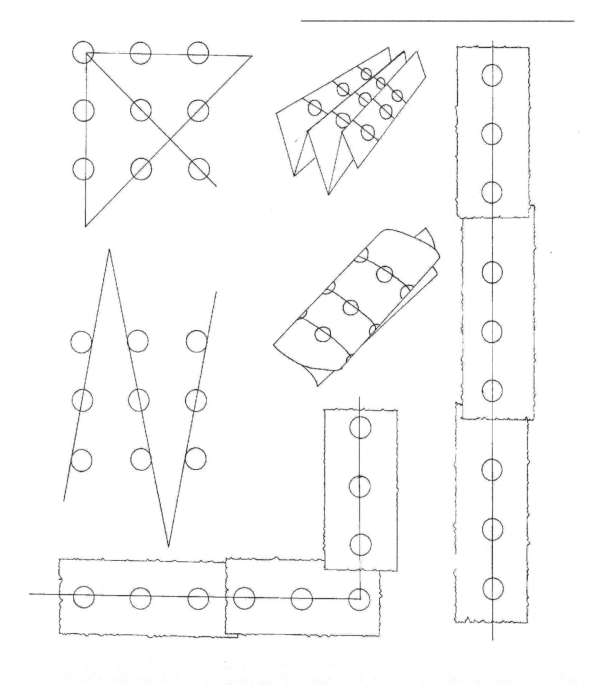

# Bibliography

I have come to the firm belief that in this day and age, and with the responsibility they have, coaches have to be more than an empty vessel, a mirror, or a slave to their clients' agenda. They should be well informed and up to date with global affairs and trends, especially about environmental and economic degradation, social justice and social distress, psychotherapy and spirituality. That is a tall order, so I have just added a few books to my recommended bibliography covering these broader realms. I have deliberately avoided adding any new books on coaching, for there are too many to list and most have much to offer. My emphasis here is on broadening the vision of coaches, managers, and leaders beyond the conventional boundaries of coaching.

Barrett, Richard (1998) *Liberating the Corporate Soul*, Butterworth-Heinemann

Barrett, Richard (2006) *Building a Values-Driven Organization*, Elsevier.

Colvin, Geoff (2008) *Talent Is Overrated*, Nicholas Brealey.

Gallwey, Timothy (1986) *The Inner Game of Tennis*, Pan.

Gallwey, Timothy (1986) *The Inner Game of Golf*, Pan.

Gallwey, Timothy (2000) *The Inner Game of Work*, Texere.

Gladwell, Malcolm (2000) *The Tipping Point*, Little, Brown.

Gladwell, Malcolm (2008) *Outliers*, Little, Brown.

Goleman, Daniel (1996) *Emotional Intelligence*, Bloomsbury.

Goleman, Daniel (1999) *Working with Emotional Intelligence*, Bloomsbury.

Goleman, Daniel (2006) *Social Intelligence*, Random House.

Hartmann, Thom (1998) *The Last Hours of Ancient Sunlight*, Three Rivers Press.

Hawken, Paul, Lovins, Amory B. & Lovins, Hunter (2000) *Natural Capitalism*, Earthscan.

Hawken, Paul (2007) *Blessed Unrest*, Viking.

Hemery, David (1991) *Sporting Excellence*, Collins Willow.

James, Oliver (2008) *The Selfish Capitalist*, Vermilion.

Knight, Sue (2002) *NLP at Work*, Nicholas Brealey.

Landsberg, Max (1997) *The Tao of Coaching*, HarperCollins.

Monbiot, George (2006) *Heat*, Penguin.

Nicholas, Michael (2008) *Being the Effective Leader*, Michael Nicholas.

Perkins, John (2007) *The Secret History of the American Empire*, Dutton.

Pilger, John (1998) *Hidden Agendas*, Vintage.

Roddick, Anita (2001) *Business as Unusual*, Thorsons.

Semler, Ricardo (2001) *Maverick*, Random House.

Senge, Peter, Scharmer, C. Otto, Jaworski, Joseph & Flowers, Betty Sue (2004) *Presence*, Nicholas Brealey.

Spackman, Kerry (2009) *The Winner's Bible*, forthcoming.

Speth, James (2008) *The Bridge at the Edge of the World*, Yale University Press.

Tolle, Eckhart (2001) *The Power of Now*, Mobius.

Tolle, Eckhart (2005) *A New Earth*, Penguin.

Whitmore, Diana (1999) *Psychosynthesis Counselling in Action*, Sage.

Whitworth, Laura, House, Henry & Sandahl, Philip (1998) *Co-Active Coaching*, Davies-Black.

Zohar, Danah & Marshall, Ian (2001) *SQ: Spiritual Intelligence*, Bloomsbury.

# Acknowledgments

Any book of this nature will be the product of the author's exposure to and learning from many experiences and many people. Tim Gallwey must undoubtedly head the list as the creator of the Inner Game, the bedrock of the finest coaching. In earlier editions of this book I identified many other contributors and supporters. I will not repeat their names here, but rather draw attention to those who have influenced me during the run-up to this extended edition.

This book is the product of more years of coaching experience, of course, but more importantly of my more recent exploration of evolutionary trends in human attitudes, beliefs and behaviors, and in consciousness itself. Two people in particular enabled that. David Brown, my CEO at PCI, singled me out, kicked me off my easy chair of life, challenged my reservations, and projected me into the unlimited arena of new possibilities and into many countries all over the world. Then there is Niran Jiang, the pole star in my sky. She is my partner in the Institute of Human Excellence, PCI's Australasian strategic partner. She is a brilliant mind, a fearless role model, a teacher of many things, a well of joy and humor, a dear friend, and my utterly ruthless coach from whom there is nothing to hide and no escape. That is real coaching.

Then I want to thank the literally thousands of people I have met in the coaching profession who have had faith in the role I have attempted to play in promoting the emerging significance of coaching within all our institutions and lives, particularly in these troubled times. I feel humbled by the awards you have given me, including an Honorary Doctorate from the University of East London that came as a total surprise to someone who had always seen university education, let alone a degree, as being well out of reach.

Finally, a special thanks to Nick Brealey and his team who have given me feedback, encouragement, criticism, and suggestions that have made this fourth edition far more comprehensive than it might otherwise have been.

For information about Performance
Consultants International and the
Performance Coach Training, Performance
Coaching, Leadership and Team
Development programs and services
provided by John Whitmore and his
associates, please contact:

David Brown, Chief Executive Officer
Performance Consultants International

Direct: +44 (0)792 1360 343
Office: +44 (0)207 3736 431

Email: davidbrown@performanceconsultants.com
Website: www.performanceconsultants.com

ALSO FROM NICHOLAS BREALEY PUBLISHING

# Co-Active Coaching
## *New Skills for Coaching People Toward Success in Work and Life*

Second Edition

Laura Whitworth, Karen Kimsey-House,
Henry Kimsey-House & Phillip Sandahl

With the first edition of *Co-Active Coaching*, Laura Whitworth and her pioneering co-authors set the stage for what has become a cultural and business phenomenon—and helped launch the professional practice of coaching. Durable and flexible, their Co-Active Coaching model has stood the test of time as a transformative communication process that co-workers and teammates, direct reports and managers, teachers and students can use to build strong, collaborative relationships.

Already used as the definitive resource in dozens of corporate and professional development programmes, this new edition of *Co-Active Coaching* includes the latest terminology and a wide-ranging set of fresh coaching examples drawn from the authors' first-hand experience with thousands of international coaching trainees and clients. The power-packed Coach's Toolkit has been expanded to include more than 35 exercises, questionnaires, checklists and reproducible forms. And a CD containing sample audio coaching sessions and printable forms from the Toolkit has been added to make these proven principles and techniques both practical and immediately actionable.

**Laura Whitworth, Karen Kimsey-House and Henry Kimsey-House** are internationally recognized pioneers in the coaching field and co-founders of The Coaches Training Institute (CTI), one of the world's largest coach training organizations providing a highly regarded certification programme. **Phillip Sandahl** is a senior faculty member of CTI and cofounder of Team Coaching International.
www.thecoaches.com

ISBN 978-0-89106-198-4
Davies-Black